P9-DDT-134

CONTEMPORARY'S

English Connections

GRAMMAR FOR COMMUNICATION

BOOK 1

ISABEL KENTENGIAN

Project Editor
Charlotte Ullman

CONTEMPORARY
BOOKS
CHICAGO

Library of Congress Cataloging-in-Publication Data

English connections.
    Cover title: Contemporary's English connections.
    Bk. 1 has statement of responsibility: Isabel
Kentengian ; bk. 2: Linda Lee ; bk. 3: Catherine Porter and Elizabeth Minicz
    1. English language—Textbooks for foreign speakers.
I. Kentengian, Isabel.   II. Lee, Linda, 1950–
III. Title: Contemporary's English connections.
PE1128.L42   1993   428.2'4   93-22804
    ISBN 0-8092-4205-2 (bk. 1 : pbk.)
    ISBN 0-8092-4206-0 (bk. 2)
    ISBN 0-8092-4207-9 (bk. 3)

To ESL students and professionals, who work to
bridge cultural differences; and to my husband,
Mark, and sons, Alex and Michael.
May our world come to value its diversity.

Copyright © 1993 by Isabel Kentengian
All rights reserved

No part of this publication may be reproduced, stored in
a retrieval system, or transmitted in any form or by any
means without the prior written permission of the
publisher.

Published by Contemporary Books, Inc.
Two Prudential Plaza, Chicago, Illinois 60601-6790
Manufactured in the United States of America
International Standard Book Number: 0-8092-4205-2
10   9   8   7   6   5   4   3

Published simultaneously in Canada by
Fitzhenry & Whiteside
195 Allstate Parkway
Markham, Ontario L3R 4T8 Canada

Editorial Director
Mark Boone

Editorial
Craig Bolt
Lisa Black
Elena Anton Delaney
Eunice Hoshizaki
Lynn McEwan
Marietta Urban

Editorial Assistant
Maggie McCann

Editorial Production Manager
Norma Fioretti

Production Editor
Thomas D. Scharf

Cover Design
Georgene Sainati

Illustrators
William Colrus
Jeff Weyer
Guy Wolek

Art & Production
Sue Springston
Jan Geist
Todd Petersen

Typography
Ellen Kollmon

Cover Photograph
© Mike Yamashita,
The Image Bank

Special thanks to Caren Van Slyke

Contents

Acknowledgments

Diane Larsen-Freeman
Chief Consultant
Master of Arts in Teaching (MAT) Program
School for International Training, Brattleboro, Vermont

Judy Hanlon, Oxnard Adult School, Oxnard, California
Renee Klosz, Lindsey Hopkins Technical Education Center, Miami,
  Florida
Mohammed Iqbal, San Francisco Community College, San Francisco,
  California
Suzanne Leibman, College of Lake County, Grayslake, Illinois
Fatiha Makloufi, Community Development Agency, New York, New York
Sharon O'Malley, Region IV Educational Service Center, Houston, Texas
Catherine Porter, Adult Education Service Center, Des Plaines, Illinois
Betsy Rubin, Chicago, Illinois

Introduction

English Connections: Grammar for Communication is a three-level series for beginning to low-intermediate adult learners of English as a second language. It integrates a developmental grammar syllabus with real-life contexts within the framework of the communicative approach to language teaching.

The goal of this series is to help language learners use grammar accurately, meaningfully, and appropriately so that they can communicate effectively outside the classroom.

The inspiration behind *English Connections* is Diane Larsen-Freeman's framework for teaching grammar. It focuses on the three dimensions of grammar: form, meaning, and use. All three dimensions are equally important. Throughout this series, information on form, meaning, and use is presented whenever appropriate.

Grammar points that naturally occur together are presented and practiced within meaningful contexts through activities that are student-centered and highly interactive. Useful vocabulary relating to the contexts is also integrated into the lessons. The purpose of this series is to encourage grammatical accuracy within useful contexts that promote real communication in English. This is grammar for communication.

The Form/Meaning/Use Framework of *English Connections*

This series pushes beyond a focus on form to include the dimensions of meaning and use as well. What do we mean by these terms? Let's look at an example from Book 1. Contractions with *be* are introduced in Unit 2.

How are contractions with *be* formed?

The form of contractions is described visually in a paradigm in the grammar box. (For example, *he + is = he's* and *Chan + is = Chan's*.)

What do contractions with *be* mean?

The contracted forms of *be* have the same meaning as the full forms.

When are contractions with *be* used?

The contracted forms of *be* are used mostly in speaking but also in informal writing—for example, in a letter to a friend. Accordingly, throughout *English Connections* contracted forms are always used in conversations and informal writing; in formal situations, full forms are used. A section of Unit 2 is devoted to helping learners understand when full forms are used and when contractions are used. In this way, learners are encouraged from the beginning to use contracted forms when appropriate.

Learning when to use contractions with *be* is probably the most difficult part to learn. Even more advanced learners of English often continue to use full forms when the contracted forms are more appropriate.

Teaching a grammar point involves teaching not only the form but the meaning and use as well. Information on form, meaning, and use for each grammar point is provided in detail in the *English Connections Teacher's Edition, Book 1*, especially on the Grammar Guide page that precedes the step-by-step teaching suggestions for each unit.

Learning a Second Language

People learn a second language in many different ways. For example, visual learners learn best by looking at graphic representations of concepts. Auditory learners learn best by listening to explanations. Kinesthetic/tactile learners learn best by manipulating objects and moving around.

English Connections addresses a variety of learning styles. *Book 1* features graphic icons that represent directions to visual learners. In addition, grammar boxes are designed to aid visual learners. Listening exercises along with pair and small-group activities encourage auditory learners. Total Physical Response (TPR) activities such as "Simon Says" and other language-learning games involving movement appeal to kinesthetic/tactile learners.

Language learning is a gradual process. People do not learn everything about a grammar point before going on to the next one. Rather, they learn about its form, meaning, and use little by little and eventually put all the pieces together. In *English Connections*, only one part of a grammar point is presented at a time. In this way, grammar points are recycled for continuous practice. More information about form, meaning, and use unfolds as learners gain familiarity with grammar points. Finally, periodic review units provide opportunities for practice in freer, less structured real-life contexts.

About the Series

English Connections: Grammar for Communication consists of:

- Three student books
- Three teacher's editions
- Three workbooks
- Two audiocassettes for each level of the series

Each student book has fifteen units, five review units, a teacher script for listening exercises, an appendix with mini-exercises, and an answer key.

Each teacher's edition includes a detailed scope-and-sequence chart and full-page representations from the student book with cues for the workbook. Each unit contains a Grammar Guide page with useful background information about each grammar point, step-by-step teaching suggestions, extension activities, and a complete answer key.

Each workbook provides extended focused practice for grammar and vocabulary from each unit in the student book.

The audiocassettes include all listening exercises (also in the teacher script), all dialogues other than writing exercises, and most of the Connections and Small Talk sections.

Teaching *English Connections*

Throughout each unit, gray bars are used to signal a logical stopping point in the text. This feature can be useful in planning classroom time.

Opening Illustrations

Each unit opens with an illustration that provides a natural setting for the grammar points and vocabulary of the unit.

Elicit from students as much language as you can about the picture. Ask questions about the people and encourage students to guess what is happening.

Setting the Scene

This regular feature consists of a short conversation using authentic language that provides a context for the grammar points of the unit.

Introduce the characters in the conversation. Then read the conversation aloud a few times as naturally as possible. Have students practice it in pairs and listen to them practice.

Their pronunciation may not be perfect at this time. Don't correct every mistake you hear—this may cause students to become hesitant to speak English. Instead, write down one or two common mistakes that you may hear. Then tell the class as a group to repeat the correct pronunciation after you and encourage accuracy on those points.

Grammar Boxes

Grammatical terms are kept to a minimum throughout *English Connections*. The grammar boxes include many examples, and students are encouraged to guess the rule.

Choose examples from the box and write them on the board. Elicit more examples from the students. After giving many examples, elicit the rule from the students or, if necessary, present it in your own words. After presenting the grammar point orally, use the grammar box as a summary of the form/meaning/use information. (The teacher's editions provide step-by-step teaching suggestions for presenting each grammar point.)

The presentation of each grammar point is followed by a combination of focused and communicative practice. The goal is to help students learn to use the grammar for communication.

Focus on Vocabulary

The most effective way to learn grammar is in a meaningful context. Relevant vocabulary is introduced to develop a meaningful context.

Bring in realia (real objects) or draw pictures on the board to illustrate words. Ask questions using the words in the box. Have students actively work with new vocabulary (for example, by categorizing, comparing, or contrasting words or ideas).

Connections

This feature occurs in *Book 1* as the need arises. It helps students develop strategies for communicating in a second language and is followed by activities that allow students to practice the strategy.

Model the strategy with a more advanced student.

Small Talk

This feature presents a natural conversation that incorporates a grammar point from the unit and is followed by an activity that allows students to practice the language.

Model the conversation with a more advanced student.

Partnerwork

This feature is a two-page information-gap activity. Students work together in pairs. Each person has information that his or her partner does not have and each person should look at his or her own page only. Students work together to obtain the information orally from their partners to complete their task.

Try to pair more advanced students with those who need extra practice. Have pairs of students compare their answers in a class session.

Use What You Know

This feature is a communicative activity that involves all four skills (listening, speaking, reading, and writing) and is based on a context from the unit.

In Your Own Words

This feature provides an opportunity for more communicative practice. Students work in pairs or small groups to complete an oral and/or written task involving their own personal information.

Wrapping Up

The final feature of the unit, Wrapping Up provides a summary practice with the most important grammar points presented in the unit.

Review Units

Periodic Review Units provide opportunities for freer, more communicative practice. Review Units are cumulative, and present previously introduced grammar points in interesting, new contexts.

Teacher Script for Listening Exercises

Some grammar points are hard to distinguish in normal conversation. ("Was it singular or plural? Was it present or past tense?") Several listening exercises are included that relate to the grammar points presented. Students are asked to listen to the teacher and mark the answer that they hear.

Refer to the Teacher Script on page 159. Be sure to read the teacher script as naturally as possible, allowing for the particular needs of your students.

Appendix

The Appendix provides detailed information along with mini-exercises on pronunciation and spelling of selected grammar points. It also includes useful vocabulary, such as titles of address, common first and last names in the United States, and countries and nationalities.

Answer Key

Answers for all written exercises are provided in the Answer Key beginning on page 175. Each teacher's edition includes a complete answer key for all the exercises in the corresponding student book.

Successful Language Learning

Language learning is enhanced when students are actively and cheerfully engaged in the learning process. Sometimes students may prefer not to offer personal information about themselves. Sensitivity to their feelings is the best guide. Let students know that they can use fictitious information if they prefer.

The most important factor for success is to create a classroom atmosphere in which learning is enjoyable and relatively stress free, so students feel safe yet challenged. Happy teaching!

> Look for grammar-guide pages, step-by-step teaching suggestions, and extension activities, in *English Connections Book 1 Teacher's Edition*.

Unit 1 What's your name?

Talk about the picture. What do you see? What are they saying?

Setting the Scene

Chan: Hi. My name's *Chan*.
Teresa: Hello. I'm *Teresa*.

 1 Introduce yourself to three people. Use the model above and your own name.

 2 Introduce yourself to three different people. Use the model below and your own name.

Ewa: Hello. My name's *Ewa*.
Young-Soon: Hi. I'm *Young-Soon*.
Ewa: Glad to meet you.
Young-Soon: Nice to meet you.

 3 Talk to the people in your class. Use the model below and your own information. Can you remember people's names and their native countries?

Pedro: Hi. My name's *Pedro*.
Abdul: Hello. I'm *Abdul*.
Pedro: Where are you from?
Abdul: I'm from *Egypt*. And you?
Pedro: I'm from *Peru*.

Subject Pronouns

I

I'm from Texas.

We

We're from the United States.

You

You're from Thailand.

You

You're from Asia.

He

He's from Vietnam.

She

She's from Thailand.

It

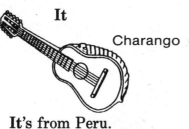

Charango

It's from Peru.

They

They're from Asia.

You can mean one person or more than one person.

4   Find a partner. Fill in the blanks together.

1. A: Where's Teresa from?
    B: ___She___'s from Texas.

2. A: Where's Pedro from?
    B: _____'s from Peru.

3. A: Where are Chan and Young-Soon from?
    B: _____'re from Asia. Chan is from Vietnam and Young-Soon is from Korea.

4. B: Where's Ewa from?
    A: _____'s from Poland.

5. B: Where's Abdul from?
    A: _____'s from Egypt.

6. B: _____'m from _____.
        Where are you from?
    A: _____'m from _____.

Focus on Vocabulary

The Alphabet

Aa	Bb	Cc	Dd	Ee	Ff	Gg	Hh	Ii	Jj	Kk	Ll	Mm
Nn	Oo	Pp	Qq	Rr	Ss	Tt	Uu	Vv	Ww	Xx	Yy	Zz

5 Circle the letter you hear.

1. a e	2. d t	3. m n	4. g j
5. b d	6. c s	7. o u	8. b v

6 This is Teresa Ortega.

What is your first name?

My first name is _____.

What is your last name?

My last name is _____.

Her **first name** is Teresa.
Her **last name** is Ortega.

7 Your teacher will spell six common American last names. Write them below. Then check your answers in the Appendix on page 163.

1. _____	4. _____
2. _____	5. _____
3. _____	6. _____

8 Talk to two people. Ask, "What's a common last name in *Ecuador*?" If you need to, ask, "How do you spell that, please?" Write your answers in the chart below.

Country	Common Last Names
Ecuador	Gómez

Please Spell That

Work with a partner. One person will be Person A. The other will be Person B. If you are Person A, look at this page only. If you are Person B, turn the page and look at page 6 only.

What are some popular names for babies in the U.S.?
Person B will tell you about some popular names for girls. Write the names on the signs.

Tell Person B about some popular names for boys. Help your partner spell the names.

Here is one way to do it.

A: Look at baby number 7. What's *her* name?
B: *Jessica.*
A: Please spell that.
B: *J-E-S-S-I-C-A.*

Write *Jessica* on sign number 7.

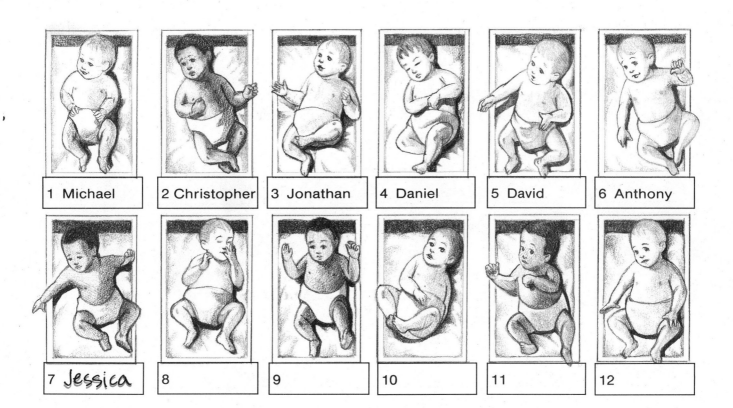

1 Michael   2 Christopher   3 Jonathan   4 Daniel   5 David   6 Anthony

7 Jessica   8   9   10   11   12

Please Spell That

Work with a partner. One person will be Person A. The other will be Person B. If you are Person A, look at page 5 only. If you are Person B, look at this page only.

What are some popular names for babies in the U.S.?
Person A will tell you about some popular names for boys. Write the names on the signs.

Tell Person A about some popular names for girls. Help your partner spell the names.

Here is one way to do it.

B: Look at baby number *1*. What's *his* name?
A: *Michael.*
B: Please spell that.
A: *M-I-C-H-A-E-L.*

Write *Michael* on sign number 1.

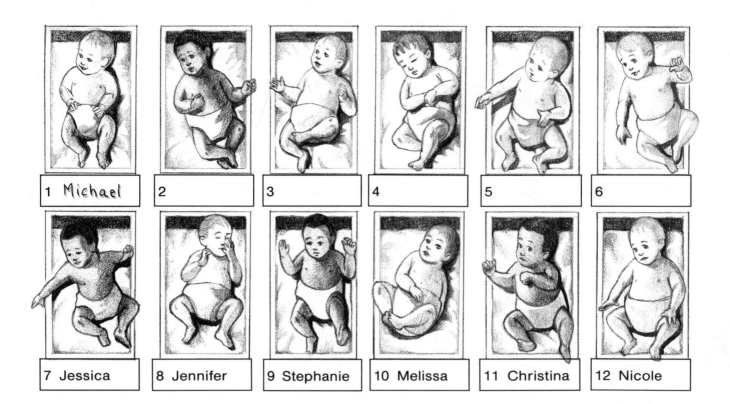

1 Michael   2   3   4   5   6

7 Jessica   8 Jennifer   9 Stephanie   10 Melissa   11 Christina   12 Nicole

Saying Hello and Saying Good-bye

"Hi."   "Hello."   "Goodbye."   "Bye."

"Good morning."   "Good afternoon."   "Good evening."

"See you later."   "Good night."

 9 Find a partner. Make some conversations. Use your own names.

Pedro: Hello/Hi/Good morning/Good afternoon/Good evening, *Abdul*.
Abdul: Hello/Hi/Good morning/Good afternoon/Good evening, *Pedro*.

Abdul: Good-bye/Bye/Good night/See you later, *Pedro*.
Pedro: Good-bye/Bye/Good night/See you later, *Abdul*.

Talk to five people. Ask them the questions below. Write the answers in the chart. Remember to ask, "Please spell that."

Ask:	Answer:
What's your first name?	*Ewa.*
What's your last name?	*Boksa.*
Where are you from?	I'm from *Poland.*

	First Name	Last Name	Native Country
	Ewa	Boksa	Poland
1.			
2.			
3.			
4.			
5.			

Wrapping Up

Sit in a circle. Follow the model below. Tell the name and native country of the people who spoke before you. Then add your own name and native country. The last person talks about everyone!

♦ Present of *Be*
(Statements and Negative
Statements)
♦ Contractions with *Be*
♦ *Be* + Adjective
♦ Contractions and Full Forms

Unit 2 Nice to meet you

Talk about the picture. Where are they? What are they doing?

Setting the Scene

Ana: Hi everyone! Sorry I'm late.
Teresa: That's OK. How are you?
Ana: Fine.
Teresa: Ana, this is Chan.
         He's in my English class.
         He's from Vietnam.
Ana: Nice to meet you.
Chan: Nice to meet you too.

Present of *Be* (Statements)

am	is	are
I **am** from Vietnam. **I'm** from Vietnam.	Chan **is** from Vietnam. She He It Chan**'s** from Vietnam.	You **are** from Vietnam. We They You**'re** from Vietnam.

> We use **am**, **is**, **are** mostly in writing. We use **'m**, **'s**, **'re** mostly in speaking.

1 Fill in the blanks. Use _am_, _is_, or _are_.

> Juana,
>
> Let me tell you about the people in my English class. They ___are___ from many countries. I think I _____ the only person from the United States. Young-Soon, Ewa, and Sumalee _____ the women in my class. Young-Soon _____ from Korea. Ewa _____ from Poland. Sumalee _____ from Thailand. Anton, Pedro, Chan, and Abdul _____ the men in my class. Anton _____ Russian, Pedro _____ Peruvian, Chan _____ Vietnamese, and Abdul _____ Egyptian. My teacher _____ from Chicago. My class is fun.
>
> *Teresa*

2 Write about yourself. Tell the class.

My name _____ _____. I _____ from _____.

Contractions with *Be*

I	+	am	=	I'm
You	+	are	=	You're
He	+	is	=	He's
She	+	is	=	She's
It	+	is	=	It's
We	+	are	=	We're
They	+	are	=	They're
Chan	+	is	=	Chan's
My friend	+	is	=	My friend's

Contractions are used mostly in speaking and informal writing.

English speakers use many contractions when they speak.
A contraction is a short form. For example, *I am* becomes *I'm* (not I,m).
The ['] mark means a letter is missing.

3 Circle the words you hear.

1. I am   I'm   2. She is   She's   3. You are   You're

4. He is   He's   5. They are   They're   6. My friend is
                                                      My friend's

4 Talk about the students. Use the model below.

A: Who's that?
B: That's *Ewa*. *She's* from *Poland*.

Ewa

Poland

Pedro

Peru

Teresa

the United States

Young-Soon, Sumalee, and Chan

Asia

That's me.

I'm from _____.

Present of *Be* (Negative Statements)

	am not		is not		are not	
	I **am not**	from Russia.	Ewa **is not**	from Russia.	We **are not**	from Russia.
	I'**m not**		Ewa'**s not**		We'**re not**	
			She **is not**		You **are not**	
			She'**s not**		You'**re not**	
			He **is not**		They **are not**	
			He'**s not**		They'**re not**	
			It **is not**			
			It'**s not**			

> There are two negative forms for **is not** and **are not**:
>
> She'**s not**.   She **isn't**.
> They'**re not**. They **aren't**.
>
> Both are correct.

5 **The sentences below are wrong. Correct them. Use the map.**
Example: Read: Sumalee is from Lampang, Thailand.
          Say: Sumalee's not from Lampang. She's from Bangkok.

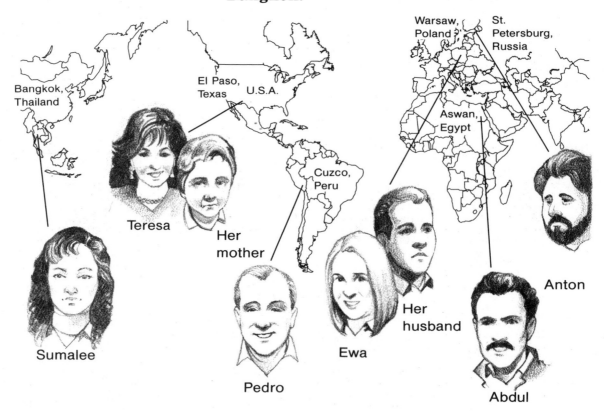

1. Sumalee is from Lampang, Thailand.
2. Teresa and her mother are from San Antonio, Texas.
3. Pedro is from Lima, Peru.
4. Ewa and her husband are from Krakow, Poland.
5. Abdul is from Cairo, Egypt.
6. Anton is from Moscow, Russia.

6 Work in small groups. Write the name of your native country on a piece of paper. Put the papers in a bag. Choose a paper from the bag. Follow the model below.

Focus on Vocabulary

Talking About *North*, *South*, *East*, and *West*

If a place is in the middle of a country or state, you can say: *Austin is in central Texas.*

7 Where are these cities in Texas? Circle the right word.

1. Amarillo is in the north / south.
2. Dallas is in the northeast / northwest.
3. Houston is in the southeast / southwest.
4. El Paso is in the east / west.

8 Find a partner. Practice the following conversation. Use your own information.

A: Where are you from?
B: I'm from *Mexico*.
A: Where are you from in *Mexico*?
B: *Monterrey*. It's in the *north*.

Be + Adjective (Nationality)

I am **Polish**.
Young-Soon is **Korean**.
Abdul is **Egyptian**.
Sumalee and Lek are **Thai**.

I'm Polish.
She's Korean.
He's Egyptian.
They're Thai.

Look at the Appendix on pages 164–165 for a list of countries and nationalities.

9 These people are also studying English. Do you know their nationalities? Look at the Appendix on page 164.

Women:
Carmen is from **Honduras**.   She is Honduran.

1. Lien is from **China**. _____

2. Yukiko and Yumi are from **Japan**. _____

3. Guadalupe and Marta are from **Guatemala**. _____

4. Judy is from **the United States**. _____

Men:
1. Armando is from **Mexico**. _____

2. Paulo and Carlos are from **Brazil**. _____

3. Jonas and Ivan are from **Ukraine**. _____

4. Mustafa is from **Syria**. _____

10 What is your nationality? _____

11 Talk to two people. Write their names and nationalities below. Can you find people from two different countries?

Name	Nationality

Be + Adjective

I **am** | cold.	Ana **is** | cold.	We **are** | cold.
I'**m**	Ana'**s**	We'**re**
	She **is**	You **are**
	She'**s**	You'**re**
	He **is**	They **are**
	He'**s**	
	It **is**	They'**re**
	It'**s**	

Use *am, is,* and *are* to connect the subject and the adjective.

Subject	Verb	Adjective
Ana	is	cold.

12 **Find a partner. Talk about the pictures below. Look at number 1. Say, "It's hot." Use these words:**

cold   hot   hungry   thirsty   tired

Contractions and Full Forms

Look at how contractions and full forms are used.

Dear Sir or Madam:

    My name is Marta Boksa. I am from Poland.

Contractions are used mostly in speaking and informal situations. Full forms are used mostly in writing and formal situations.

 13 Circle the form you think is correct.

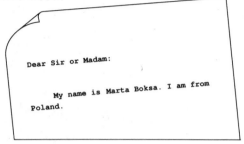

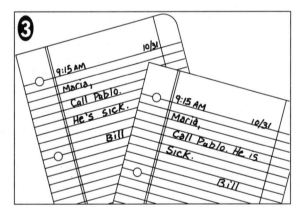

Small Talk: How are you?

People ask, "How are you?" to say hello. "How are you?" is a greeting. Most people do not want to know about a person's health. They just want to say hello.

Possible answers are: "Fine." "Good." "Great." "OK."

Connections: Introductions

Look at the Appendix on page 168 for information on using Mr., Ms., Miss, and Mrs.

 14 Work in groups of three. Practice introducing each other. Afterward, introduce your partners to the class.

 Find a partner. Read the sentences below. The sentences are about some of the largest cities in the U.S. All of the sentences are wrong. Correct them. Use the map of the U.S. above.

Example: Read: San Antonio is in New Mexico.
　　　　　Say: San Antonio's not in New Mexico. It's in Texas.

1. New York City is in New Jersey.
2. Los Angeles is in Washington.
3. Chicago is in Michigan.
4. Houston is in Arizona.
5. Philadelphia is in New York.

6. San Diego is in Nevada.
7. Detroit is in Illinois.
8. Dallas is in Florida.
9. Phoenix is in Colorado.
10. Seattle is in Oregon.

Wrapping Up

 Complete the paragraph. Write about yourself.

My name _____ _____ _____.
　　　　 (am/is/are)　　(first name)　　　　(last name)

I _____ _____. I _____
　(am/is/are)　　(nationality)　　(am/is/are)

from _____ in _____. _____
　　　(name of city)　　　(name of country)　　　(name of city)

_____ in the _____ of my native country.
(am/is/are)　　(north/south/east/west)

Unit 3 I'm new here

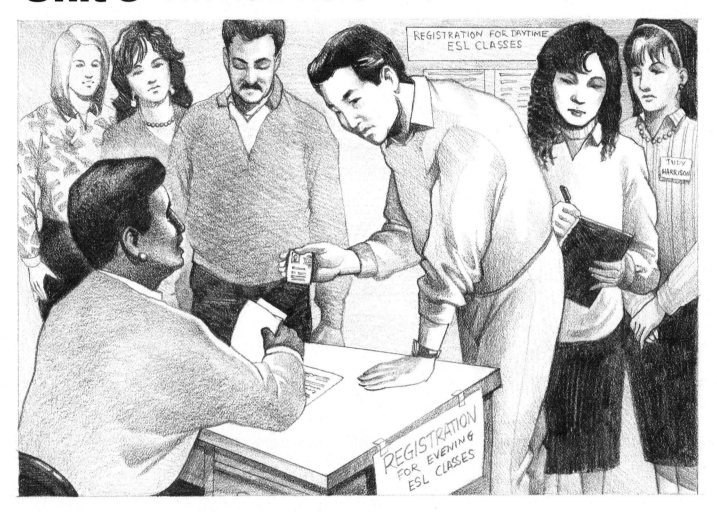

Talk about the picture. Where are they? What are they doing?

Setting the Scene

Linda Jacobs:	Hi. I'm Linda Jacobs. What's your name?
Fu Wang:	My name's Fu Wang.
Linda Jacobs:	Are you Chinese?
Fu Wang:	Yes, I am. I'm from Shanghai.
Linda Jacobs:	Are you a student here now?
Fu Wang:	No, I'm not. I'm new here.

Present of *Be* (Yes/No Questions)

In a question, the verb *be* (*am*, *is*, *are*) comes in front of the subject.

Don't forget the question mark. Put ? at the end of a question.

Statement: Pedro is from Peru.
subject verb

They are Korean.
subject verb

Question: **Is Pedro** from Peru?
verb subject

Are they Korean?
verb subject

1 **Questions sound different from statements. Can you hear the difference between a statement and a question? Check (✔) the sentence you hear.**

Shanghai is in China.   Is Shanghai in China?

1. ☐ Guatemala is in Central America.
   ☑ Is Guatemala in Central America?

2. ☐ Thailand is in Southeast Asia.
   ☐ Is Thailand in Southeast Asia?

3. ☐ Poland is next to Ukraine.
   ☐ Is Poland next to Ukraine?

4. ☐ Egypt is on the Mediterranean Sea.
   ☐ Is Egypt on the Mediterranean Sea?

5. ☐ Peru is on the Pacific Ocean.
   ☐ Is Peru on the Pacific Ocean?

6. ☐ Uganda is in Africa.
   ☐ Is Uganda in Africa?

Present of *Be* (Short Answers)

	Affirmative	Negative
Question:	Is Fu Chinese?	Is Teresa Chinese?
Short Answer:	**Yes, he is.**	**No, she's not. She's American.**
Question:	Are they students?	Are they American?
Short Answer:	**Yes, they are.**	**No, they're not.**

Do not use contractions in affirmative short answers:

~~Yes, she's.~~   ~~Yes, I'm.~~   ~~Yes, we're.~~

Yes, she is.   Yes, I am.   Yes, we are.

Contractions are fine in negative short answers.

> Remember to add a comma after Yes or No:
> Yes, I am.
> No, I'm not.

  2 **Look at the map. Listen to the question. Circle the right short answer.**

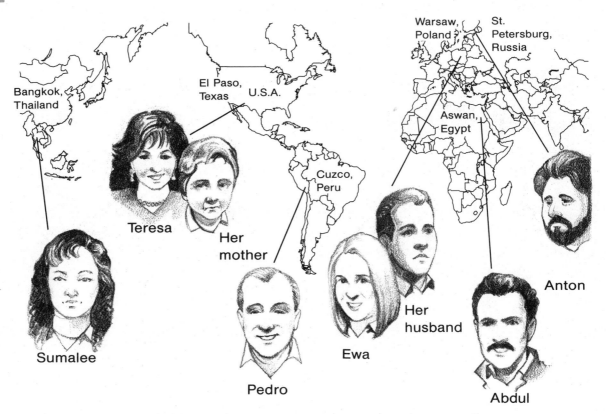

1. Yes, they are.
   No, they're not.

2. Yes, she is.
   No, she's not.

3. Yes, he is.
   No, he's not.

4. Yes, they are.
   No, they're not.

5. Yes, he is.
   No, he's not.

6. Yes, he is.
   No, he's not.

Adjectives that Describe Feelings

I'm	(I am)	happy.
You're	(You are)	sad.
She's	(She is)	scared.
He's	(He is)	confused.
We're	(We are)	proud.
They're	(They are)	angry.

Use *be* (*am*, *is*, *are*) + adjective to talk about feelings.

3 Point to the feeling you hear described.

Learning English is hard! Mi-Cha does not understand the lesson. She is **frustrated**. Muhammad worked all night. He is **tired**. Eduardo made a mistake. He is **embarrassed**. But Carmen is **proud**. She did not make any mistakes in the exercise.

4 **Look at the pictures below. Write a word that describes the feeling. Check your answers with a partner. There is one word that is not in the vocabulary box on page 22. Write it here:**

_____.

1. _____ 2. _____ 3. _____

4. _____ 5. _____ 6. _____

5 **Work in groups of three. Make nine cards. Write one feeling word on each card. Each person writes three cards. Put the cards in a pile. Take turns picking a card. Act out the word on the card. Your partners try to guess the word. Use short answers.**

Example: A: Are you angry?
B: Yes, I am. OR No, I'm not.

6 **Write one word in each blank. Find a partner. Practice the conversation.**

Sumalee: Teresa, tell me about our classmates.
Teresa: OK.

Sumalee: ___Is___ Pedro Latin American?

Teresa: Yes, ___he___ ___is___.

Sumalee: _____ _____ Colombian?

Teresa: No, _____ _____. He's from Peru.

Sumalee: _____ Chan and Young-Soon Asian?

Teresa: Yes, _____ _____. He's from Vietnam, and she's from Korea.

Sumalee: _____ Abdul Egyptian?

Teresa: Yes, _____ _____.

Sumalee: _____ you Mexican?

Teresa: No, _____ _____. I'm Mexican-American. I'm from Texas.

7 **Your teacher will read the passage.**

People often ask Teresa, "Are you Mexican?" She feels upset when this happens. Her parents are from Mexico, but she is Mexican-American. She is from Texas.

Do people try to guess where you are from?

How do you feel when this happens?

Sumalee: Excuse me.
What's this?
Judy: It's an ID card.
Sumalee: Oh. Thank you.

Use these expressions to ask what something is.

	Question	**Answer**
To ask about one thing:	**What's this?**	It's a/an _____.
To ask about two or more things:	**What are these?**	They're _____.

8 **Find a partner. This is Young-Soon's desk. Point to something. Ask, *What's this?* or *What are these?* Answer, *It's a/an* _____. OR *They're* _____ s.**

Words you will need:
an address
an area code
an ID card
registration forms
letters

a passport
a social security number
a telephone number
zip codes

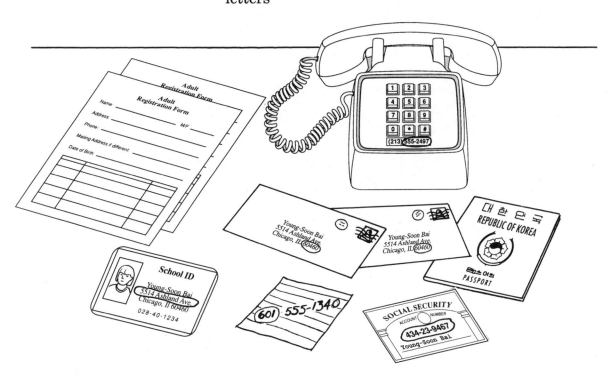

Numbers

0	1	2	3	4	5	6	7	8	9
zero (oh)	one	two	three	four	five	six	seven	eight	nine

Listen to your teacher read this dialogue.

Man: Hello.
Maria: Hello. Is this the ESL school?
Man: No, it's not. It's a gym.
Maria: Is this 535-0170?
Man: Excuse me?
Maria: Is this 535-0170?
Man: No. You have the wrong number.
Maria: I'm sorry.
Man: That's OK. Bye.
Maria: Good-bye.

9 **Practice reading these numbers aloud.**

Telephone numbers: (219) 782-0194
area code two one nine (pause)
seven eight two (pause)
oh one nine four

Zip codes: 11245
one one two four five

Social security numbers: 334-09-5431
three three four (pause)
oh nine (pause)
five four three one

10 **Write only the numbers you hear.**

1. _____   5. _____

2. _____   6. _____

3. _____   7. _____

4. _____   8. _____

Use these expressions when you do not understand something:

Excuse me?   Please repeat that.
Pardon me?   Say that again, please.

It is OK to ask people to repeat.

11 Find a partner. Practice these conversations. Add *Excuse me, Pardon me, Please repeat that,* or *Say that again, please.*

1. A: What's your address?
   B: It's 104 Broad Street.
   A: Excuse me?
   B: It's 104 Broad Street.
   A: Thank you.
   B: You're welcome.

2. A: What's your zip code?
   B: It's 60640.
   A: _Excuse me ?_
   B: It's 60640.
   A: Thank you.
   B: You're welcome.

3. A: What's your social security number?
   B: It's 098-40-1539.
   A: _____
   B: It's 098-40-1539.
   A: Thank you.
   B: You're welcome.

4. A: What's your telephone number?
   B: It's 232-4467.
   A: _____
   B: It's 232-4467.
   A: Thank you.
   B: You're welcome.

12 Work in small groups. Sit in a circle. Write your phone number on a small piece of paper. Put everyone's papers in a bag. Choose a paper from the bag. See if the number belongs to the person on your right.

Example: A: Is your phone number *(312) 802-1257?*
           B: Excuse me?
           A: Is your phone number *(312) 802-1257?*
           B: Yes, that's right. OR
               No, it's not. It's *(312) 341-5659.*

Afterward, repeat this activity. Use your address.

In Your Own Words

  Ask six people their names, addresses, and phone numbers. Write the information in the address book. Ask, "What's your name?" "What's your address?" "What's your zip code?" "What's your area code?" "What's your phone number?"

```
A
B
C      Name: _____        Name: _____
D      Address: _____        Address: _____
E      _____        _____
F      _____        _____
G      Phone Number: (    ) _____        Phone Number: (    ) _____
H                    (Area Code)                           (Area Code)
I
J
K      Name: _____        Name: _____
L      Address: _____        Address: _____
       _____        _____        M
       _____        _____        N
       Phone Number: (    ) _____        Phone Number: (    ) _____      O
                     (Area Code)                           (Area Code)          P
                                                                                Q
                                                                                R
       Name: _____        Name: _____      S
       Address: _____        Address: _____      T
       _____        _____        U
       _____        _____        V
       Phone Number: (    ) _____        Phone Number: (    ) _____      W
                     (Area Code)                           (Area Code)          X
                                                                                Y
                                                                                Z
```

Wrapping Up

 Write the missing words.

Linda: Hi. _____ Linda Jacobs. _____ your name?

Sumalee: My _____ Sumalee Thanarang.

Linda: _____ _____ Korean?

Sumalee: No, _____ _____. _____ Thai.

Work with a partner. One person will be Person A. The other will be Person B. If you are Person A, look at this page only. If you are Person B, look at page 30 only.

Some of the ID cards from the Adult ESL School are wrong. There are three mistakes in Dina Romanov's ID card. Person B has the correct information. It's on the registration form. Ask Person B the questions below. Make a new ID card with the correct information. Then Person B asks you about Kemal Ersu's ID card. You have the correct information about Kemal. It's on the registration form.

Ask these questions:

Is her name _____ ? Is her zip code _____ ?

How do you spell that? Is her telephone number _____ ?

Is her address _____ ? Is she from _____ ?

What does she do _____ ?

ID CARD
ADULT ESL PROGRAM

NAME __Romanov Dina__
      Last   First   Middle

ADDRESS __145 Chestnut Street__
      Number   Street

__Forest Park IL 60201__
City   State   Zip Code

PHONE NO. __(708) 535-2104__
      (Area Code)   Telephone

NATIVE COUNTRY __Russia__

OCCUPATION __teacher__

ID CARD
ADULT ESL PROGRAM

NAME __Romanov__
      Last   First   Middle

ADDRESS _____
      Number   Street

_____
City   State   Zip Code

PHONE NO. _____
      (Area Code)   Telephone

NATIVE COUNTRY _____

OCCUPATION _____

REGISTRATION CARD ADULT ESL CENTER
Please Print

NAME __Ersu__ __Kemal__ __Umit__
     Last   First   Middle

ADDRESS __554 Ashland Avenue__
     Number   Street

__Chicago, Il.__ __60640__   PHONE NO. __(312) 275-0104__
City   State   Zip Code   (Area Code)   Telephone

NATIVE COUNTRY __Turkey__ OCCUPATION __waiter__

Work with a partner. One person will be Person A. The other will be Person B. If you are Person B, look at this page only. If you are Person A, look at page 29 only.

Some of the ID cards from the Adult ESL School are wrong. Person A asks you about Dina Romanov's ID card. You have the correct information. It's on the registration form. There are three mistakes in Kemal Ersu's ID card. Person A has the correct information. It's on the registration form. Ask Person A the questions below. Make a new ID card with the correct information.

Ask these questions:

Is his name _____ ?   Is his zip code _____ ?

How do you spell that?   Is his telephone number _____ ?

Is his address _____ ?   Is he from _____ ?

What does he do _____ ?

**ID CARD
ADULT ESL PROGRAM**

NAME __Ersu   Kemal   Umet__
　　　　Last　　　First　　　Middle

ADDRESS __511 Ashland Avenue__
　　　　　　Number　　　　Street

__Chicago IL 60640__
City　　　　State　　Zip Code

PHONE NO. __(312) 275-0104__
　　　　　(Area Code)　　Telephone

NATIVE COUNTRY __Turkey__

OCCUPATION __mechanic__

**ID CARD
ADULT ESL PROGRAM**

NAME __Ersu__
　　　　Last　　　First　　　Middle

ADDRESS _____
　　　　　　Number　　　　Street

_____
City　　　　State　　Zip Code

PHONE NO. _____
　　　　　(Area Code)　　Telephone

NATIVE COUNTRY _____

OCCUPATION _____

REGISTRATION CARD ADULT ESL CENTER
Please Print

NAME __Romanov   Dina__
　　　Last　　　　First　　　Middle

ADDRESS __145 Chester Street__
　　　　　Number　　　　Street

__Forest Park, Il.   60202__
City　　　　　State　　　Zip Code

PHONE NO. __(708) 535-2104__
　　　　　(Area Code)　　Telephone

NATIVE COUNTRY __Russia__   OCCUPATION __Cashier__

Unit 4 What do you do?

Talk about the picture. What do you see? What are they saying?

Setting the Scene

Abdul: What do you do, *Pedro*?
Pedro: I'm *an auto mechanic*.
Abdul: Oh. I'm *a taxi driver*.

1   Draw a line from each sentence to the correct picture.

1. Sumalee is a **student**.

a.

2. Ewa is a **homemaker**.

b.

3. Young-Soon is a **nurse's aide**.

c.

4. Abdul is a **taxi driver**.

d.

5. Anton is an **electrician**.

e.

Connections: Asking for Information

2 **Match the job to its explanation. Then find a partner. Talk about the jobs. Use the model above. Add your own job and its explanation.**

auto mechanic   someone who cleans and fixes things in a building

babysitter   someone who takes care of other people's children

janitor   someone who fixes cars

_____ _____

Indefinite Articles: *A* and *An*

Use **an** before words that begin with vowel sounds. *A, e, i, o, u* are vowels. Words that begin with a silent *h* (like *hour*) also use **an**.

a student

~~a~~ students

Use *a* before most words: **a teacher**
a pilot

Use *an* before words that begin with a vowel sound: **an electrician**
an artist

3 Put *A(a)* or *An(an)* before each job and workplace.

Example: __A__ secretary and __a__ clerk work in __an__ office.

1. ____ teacher works in ____ school.

2. ___ aide, ___ nurse, and ___ doctor all work in ___ hospital.

3. ___ hairstylist works in ___ hair salon, but ___ barber works in ___ barber shop.

4. ___ waiter, ___ busboy, ___ cook and ___ dishwasher all work in ___ restaurant.

5. ___ electrician, ___ plumber, ___ carpenter, ___ architect, and ___ painter all work at ___ construction site.

4   Copy the job under the correct workplace. Remember to use _a_ or _an_.

architect	cook	hairstylist	~~secretary~~
busboy	dishwasher	nurse	teacher
carpenter	doctor	nurse's aide	waiter
~~clerk~~	electrician	plumber	waitress

a secretary
a clerk

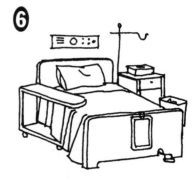

Singular and Plural Nouns

Singular (one)	Plural (two or more)
a student	students
a daycare worker	daycare workers
an artist	artists
an electrician	electricians

She is **a student**.   They are **electricians**.

Add *-s* to most nouns to make them plural.

> Do not use **a** or **an** with a plural noun.

  5 Listen to the words your teacher will read. Are they singular or plural? Circle A or B.

1. a. daycare   b. daycare   3. a. student   b. students
   workers   worker

2. a. nurse   b. nurses   4. a. cooks   b. cook

 6 Look at the pictures. If the words should be singular, add *a* or *an*. If they should be plural, add an *-s*.

1. _a_ truck   2. ___ doctor___   3. ___ waitress___
   driver___

4. ___ auto mechanic___   5. ___ carpenter___   6. ___ ___

7   Write a sentence about each picture. Follow the example.

dancer

1. *They are dancers.*

teacher

2. _____

plumber

3. _____

pilot

4. _____

Connections: What do you do?

In the United States, people ask "What do you do?" when they meet a new person. They want to know what your job is.

You can answer: "I'm *a clerk*." OR you can say **where** you work.

I work at a hotel.
    at a factory.
    at a store.
    at home.

You can say, "I'm not working now" if you are unemployed.

8   Find a partner. Talk about yourself. Use the model below.

Abdul: Hi. My name's *Abdul.*
Pedro: Hello. I'm *Pedro*. Nice to meet you.
Abdul: What do you do?
Pedro: I'm *an auto mechanic.* What do you do?
Abdul: I'm *a taxi driver.*

"Hi."   "Hello."

Use What You Know

Work in groups of three. Make nine cards. Each person takes three cards and writes a different job on each card. Put the nine cards in a pile. Then take turns picking one card at a time and asking a question about it. Follow the model below. Answer truthfully!

In Your Own Words

Find three classmates. Ask about their jobs and where they work. Put the information in the chart below. Use this model:

Ewa: What do you do, Young-Soon?

Young-Soon: I'm a nurse's aide.

Ewa: Oh. Where do you work?

Young-Soon: Washington Hospital.

Ewa: That's interesting.

Name	Job	Place of Work
Young-Soon	nurse's aide	hospital
Ewa	homemaker	home
1.		
2.		
3.		

Wrapping Up

Look at the pictures. Try to guess what the jobs are. Write your questions on the lines. Then ask a partner your questions. Take turns asking and answering questions. Then check your answers below.

A: Are they *dancers*?
B: Yes, they are.
    OR
No, they're not.
They're *actors*.

Write: _Are they dancers?_

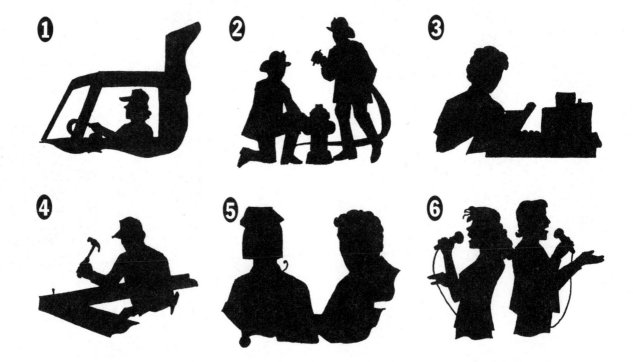

1. _____   4. _____

2. _____   5. _____

3. _____   6. _____

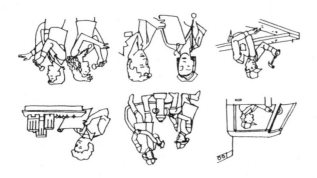

Unit 5 What's this?

What do you see in the picture? What do you see in your classroom?

Setting the Scene

Abdul: Excuse me, Ewa.
                   What's that?
Ewa: Oh, this is a notebook.

Demonstratives: *This/That/These/Those*

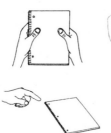

	Singular	Plural
Near	**This** is a notebook.	**These** are notebooks.
Far	**That's** a notebook.	**Those** are notebooks.

That is becomes **that's**. The other forms cannot be contracted.

Use *this/these* to show that something is near.
Use *that/those* to show that something is far.

1   **What is Ewa saying? Circle the correct answer.**

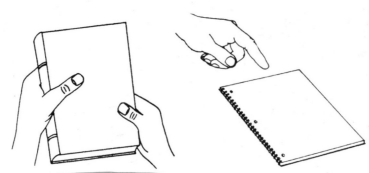

1. This is a book.
   That's a book.

2. This is a notebook.
   That's a notebook.

3. This is a pen.
   That's a pen.

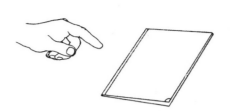

4. This is a folder.

5. This is a piece of paper.

6. This is an eraser.

That's a folder.

That's a piece of paper.

That's an eraser.

2 **What is in a classroom? Write sentences with *this, that, these,* or *those*. When you need to, add an *-s* or add *a* or *an*. Use these words:**

blackboard   clock   light

chair   desk   shelf

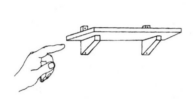      

1. That is a shelf.   2. _____   3. _____

   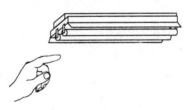   

4. _____   5. _____   6. _____

	Singular	**Plural**
Near	What's this?	What are these?
Far	What's that?	What are those?

In the U.S., people expect you to ask questions when you do not know something.

3 Find a partner. Guess what the numbered objects are.

Example: Ask, "What's this?" "What's that?" "What are these?" or "What are those?"

Answer, "I think it's a **pen**." or "I think they're **pens**."

Now check your answers.
How many did you guess correctly?

4 **Your teacher will cover an object with a piece of cloth. Touch the object through the cloth. Guess what it is. Take turns.**

Say, "This is a _____" OR

"These are _____s" when

you know what the object is.

Say, "I **think** this is a

_____" OR "I **think** these

are _____s" when you are

not sure what the object is.

Then, do the same exercise
in groups of three or four.

5 **Find a partner. Together, make eight cards. Write one of the words below on each card.**

| a blackboard | a book bag | a desk | a notebook |
| a book | a clock | an eraser | a pen |

Put the cards face down on a desk. Guess what each card is. If you are near the card, say, "I think **this** is *a pen*." If you are far from the card, say, "I think **that**'s *a pen*." Then look at the card.

6 **Look at the pictures and write sentences. Follow the model. Use** *long, new, light, easy,* **and** *large.*

Those pencils are long.

That problem is hard.

That clock is small.

Classroom Commands

Copy the correct command on the line. Check your answers with a classmate.

Circle the word.   Listen.
Close the book.   Open the book.
Hand in/Turn in your homework.   Repeat the word.

7   Work in groups of three or four. Play "Simon Says." One person will be Simon. Simon will say, "Simon says 'Close your book.'" Pretend to close your book. If Simon says "Close your book" only and does not say "Simon says," do not do anything.
    Take turns being Simon.

Be + Adjective + Noun

This suitcase is light. ⟶ This is a light suitcase.
  noun   adjective   adjective noun

These suitcases are light. ⟶ These are light suitcases.
  noun   adjective   adjective noun

> Do not add
> -s to an adjective.

Most adjectives have almost the same meaning before the noun and after the noun.

8 **Look at Exercise 6 again. Change the sentences. Follow the example.**

Example: Those pencils are long. _Those are long pencils._

1. _____ 3. _____

2. _____ 4. _____

Focus on Vocabulary

Descriptive Adjectives

expensive	cheap	clean	dirty
old	new	easy	hard
thick	thin	large	small
heavy	light	short	long

Colors

black	red	yellow	blue	gray	pink
brown	orange	green	purple	white	beige

9 Find a partner. Look at the pictures. Make a sentence for each picture. Use the vocabulary words on page 48.

Example: *Those are small books.*

10 Find a partner. Talk about the things you see in your classroom. Use the vocabulary words on page 48.

Example: *This is a large desk.*

11 Work in small groups. Think of an object in your classroom. Describe it. The other people in the group try to guess what it is. Take turns.

Example: A: It's a pink object.
B: Is it that pink sweater?
A: No, it's not. It's a small object.
C: Is it this pink eraser?
A: Yes, it is. Your turn.

In Your Own Words

Bring a special object from your native country to class. Tell the class about it. What is it? Where is it from? What is it used for?

This is a *charango*. It's from Peru. It's used to play music. It's made from an armadillo.

Fill in the following chart.

What is it?	Where is it from?	What is it used for?
charango	Peru	It's used to *play music.*
		It's used to
		It's used to
		It's used to
		It's used to

Wrapping Up

What is the man saying? Make sentences about the things. Use the model.

This notebook is thick.

Review: Units 4 and 5

1 These people are famous entertainers, athletes, and artists. Do you know who they are? Work with a partner. Try to match the names and pictures. Use the example below. Then write a sentence about the picture.

Mikhail Baryshnikov   Sophia Loren

Jackie Chan   Madonna

Whoopi Goldberg   Steffi Graf and Monica Seles

Julio Iglesias   Michael Jordan and "Magic" Earvin Johnson

Example: A: Who's this? Is *she* a *dancer*?
      B: I think that's *Whoopi Goldberg. She's* a *comedian. She's* not a *dancer.*

1. dancer? comedian?

She is a comedian.

2. singer? actor?

3. actor? dancer?

4. basketball players? soccer players?

5. actor? comedian?

_____

6. comedian? actress?

_____

7. gymnasts? tennis players?

_____

8. singer? actress? dancer?

_____

2 **Think of some other famous people. Choose someone who is famous in your native country or in your part of the world. Your teacher will call on the first person. Use the model.**

Example: Teacher: Marta.
Marta: Who is *Gabriel García Márquez?*
A: Is he a *dancer?*
Marta: No, he's not a *dancer.*
B: Is he a *writer?*
Marta: Yes, he's a *writer.* He's from my country.

Unit 6 In the house

What do you see in the picture? What do you have in your kitchen?

Setting the Scene

Young-Soon's sister loves to cook. She has many kitchen appliances. There is a microwave oven, rice cooker, and toaster. They are on the counters. There is also a blender in the cabinet next to the stove.

 **1** Listen to your teacher read *Setting the Scene*. Point to the objects you hear. Are there any objects you cannot find?

Focus on Vocabulary

Kitchen Items

stove	dishes (plates)	pans	blender
refrigerator	cups	pots	rice cooker
freezer	spoons	oven	dishwasher
cabinets	knives	toaster	glasses
sink	forks	microwave oven	table

 2 Find a partner. Look at page 53. Find the things in the picture. Point to each item and say "That's a chair" or "Those are plates."

 3 Which things in the vocabulary box do you cook with? Which things do you eat with?

Things to Cook with

Stove, pans

_____

_____

_____

_____

Things to Eat with

fork, spoon

_____

_____

_____

_____

Add your own words to each list.

There is/There are

Look at the picture on page 53. Your teacher will read the sentences below.

There is   a table.   (singular)

There are   two chairs.   (plural)

Is	**there**	a cup?	Yes, there is.
		a glass?	No, there's not.
			OR No, there isn't.

Are	**there**	dishes?	Yes, there are.
		forks?	No, there are not.
			OR No, there aren't.

> **There is** becomes **there's** in conversation. **There are** cannot be contracted.

4   **Look at the picture on page 53. Answer your teacher's questions. Circle Yes or No.**

1. Yes, there is. No, there's not.

2. Yes, there is. No, there's not.

3. Yes, there are. No, there aren't.

4. Yes, there are. No, there aren't.

5. Yes, there are. No, there aren't.

6. Yes, there is. No, there's not.

7. Yes, there is. No, there's not.

8. Yes, there are. No, there aren't.

5   **Find a partner. Make sentences about Abdul's kitchen. Use *There is* and *There are*.**

Example: Read: window
Say: *There isn't a window in Abdul's kitchen.*

a refrigerator
cabinets
a microwave oven
an oven
a dishwasher
a table
a coffeemaker
a window
a toaster

6   **Find a partner. What's in your kitchen? Talk about it.**

More Plural Nouns

Add -s to most nouns to make them plural.

one spoon   two spoons

Add -es to nouns that end in -s, -sh, -ch, -z, or -x.

one dish   three dishes

Say an extra syllable with words that have -es added.

one glass   four glasses

But some nouns have special forms:
one knife   two knives

one box   two boxes

one shelf   two shelves

one match   a book of matches

Look at the Appendix pages 169–171 for information about syllables, pronouncing the plural form, and more spelling rules.

7 Listen to your teacher. Check (✔) the word you hear.

1. ☐ spoon   ☐ spoons   5. ☐ dish   ☐ dishes
2. ☐ cabinet   ☐ cabinets   6. ☐ glass   ☐ glasses
3. ☐ table   ☐ tables   7. ☐ match   ☐ matches
4. ☐ coffeemaker ☐ coffeemakers 8. ☐ knife   ☐ knives

8 Change the words from singular to plural. Then say both forms of the word.

1. table _____tables_____   6. tablecloth _____
2. fork _____   7. shelf _____
3. glass _____   8. dish _____
4. knife _____   9. box _____
5. match _____   10. house _____

9 Your teacher will let you look at ten different objects for one minute. Try to remember what they are. Then your teacher will cover them. How many can you remember in two minutes? Write them below.

a pen
_____   _____
_____   _____
_____   _____
_____   _____

Find a partner. Talk about your answers. Use *There's* or *There are*. Did you remember all ten objects?

Example: *There's a pen.*

Partnerwork   ▶ Person A

Find a partner. One person looks at the picture on this page only. The other person looks at the picture on page 58 only. There are six differences in the two pictures. What are they? Ask each other questions. Use the following model.

A: *Are there glasses* in the kitchen?
B: *Yes, there are.*
A: How many *glasses* are there?
B: *Five.*

Find a partner. One person looks at the picture on this page only. The other person looks at the picture on page 57 only. There are six differences in the two pictures. What are they? Ask each other questions. Use the following model.

A: *Are there glasses* in the kitchen?
B: *Yes, there are.*
A: How many *glasses* are there?
B: *Five.*

Prepositions of Place

Words such as *next to*, *on*, *over*, or *under* tell **where** something or somebody is.

over

behind

in front of

in

under

on/on top of

next to/beside

between

10 Circle the right word.

This is the Bai family's living room. Young-Soon is sitting [in / *on* / under]

the sofa. There is a book [on / under / in] her knee. There is a lamp [over / on / in front of]

the end table. There is a painting from Korea [on / in / over] the wall,

[on / in / over] the sofa. [On / Under / In front of] the sofa is a coffee table. The baby

is [on / under / over] the rug, [on / under / next to] the coffee table. There are glasses

[next to / under / on] the books, [on / under / next to] the coffee table. There is one large

chair [in front of / over / on top of] the windows. There is also a stereo

[in / under / on] the cabinet. The stereo is [next to / under / on] the TV.

11 Find a partner. Ask, "Where are the *books*?" Find them in the picture above. Point to them. Take turns.

books	coffee table	end table	sofa
cabinet	glasses	painting	stereo
chair	lamp	rug	TV

12 Point to what you hear.

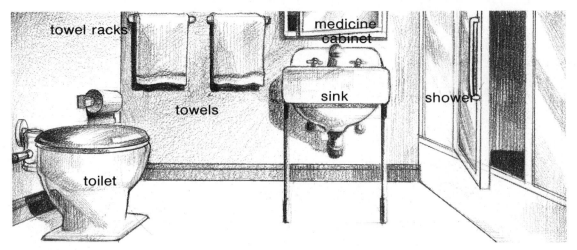

towel racks

medicine cabinet

sink

shower

towels

toilet

13 Read the following description of Abdul's bathroom.
1. Underline the words *a, an*, and *the*.
2. Then circle the word *sink* each time you see it.
3. When is *a* used before *sink*? When is *the* used before *sink*?

   This is Abdul's bathroom. There is a small sink, a brand-new toilet, a shower, and a medicine cabinet. There are two towel racks next to the sink, between the toilet and the sink. There are two towels on the towel racks. The medicine cabinet is over the sink, to the left of the shower.

Now, circle these words: toilet   shower   medicine cabinet   towel racks

Is *a/an* used the first time?   ☐ Yes   ☐ No

Is *the* used the first time?   ☐ Yes   ☐ No

Definite Article: *The*

Singular	Plural
Use *a* or *an* the first time something is talked about.	Use nothing or a number the first time something is talked about.
There is **a** glass on Abdul's sink.	There are toothbrushes in the glass.
	There are **two** toothbrushes in the glass.

Use *the* after the first time something is talked about with both singular and plural nouns.

The glass is full of water.

The glasses are full of water.

The is used with both singular and plural nouns.
    the towel
    the towels

14 **This is the bathroom in Young-Soon's apartment. Write *a, an,* or *the*.**

mirror

sink

toilet

bathtub

This is the bathroom in Young-Soon's apartment. There is ___*a*___ large sink, _____ brand-new toilet, _____ bathtub, and _____ mirror. _____ sink is next to _____ toilet. _____ bathtub is to the left of _____ sink. _____ towel rack is between _____ sink and _____ bathtub. There are four towels on it. There is _____ bath mat in front of _____ bathtub.

Use What You Know

Your teacher will show you eight different things on a table. Look at them for one minute. Then your teacher will cover the objects. Write the name of the objects in the box exactly where you see them.

Then find a partner. Talk about where things are.

Example: A: Is there a pen?
B: Yes, there is. OR No, there isn't.
A: Where is it?
B: It's between the book and the pencil.

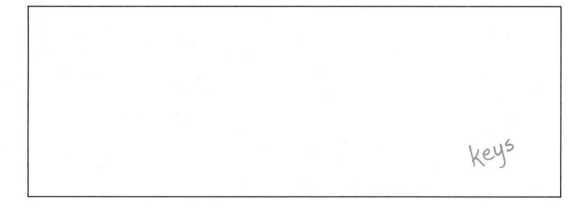

keys

In Your Own Words

Find a partner. Describe your living room to your partner. Use *there is/there are* and words such as *between, next to*, and *on*. Your partner will draw your living room. Afterward, draw your partner's living room.

Wrapping Up

Look at the picture on page 53. Circle the right word in each box.

Young-Soon's sister loves to cook. She has [a / an / the] nice kitchen and

many kitchen appliances. There is [a / an / the] rice cooker

and [a / an / the] toaster [in / on / next to] the counter [between / over / next to] the stove.

There [is / are / am] a blender [in / on / under] the cabinet [on / next to / under] [a / an / the] stove.

There [is / are / am] also [a / an / the] microwave oven [on / next to / under] [a / an / the]

refrigerator.

What appliances do you have in your kitchen? Where are they?

Unit 7 Family pictures

Who do you see in the family photograph? What do you see in the picture?

Setting the Scene

Anton: Who's that, Pedro?
Pedro: That's my wife, Gloria. These are our children—Rosa, Susana, and Juan.
Anton: And the bird?
Pedro: Oh, the bird is Susana's. Its name is Lorenzo.

Possessives of Nouns

Singular	Gloria is **Pedro's** wife.
	His **son-in-law's** name is Luis.
	Rosita is **Rosa and Luis's** daughter.
Plural	His **daughters'** names are Rosa and Susana.

> When there are two nouns, add 's to the last one only.
>
> Rosa and Luis's daughter.

1 Work with a partner. Together complete each sentence about Pedro's family.

```
                    PEDRO ─┬─ Gloria
                           │    wife
            ┌──────────────┼──────────┬────────┐
     Luis ─┬─ Rosa      Susana      Juan
son-in-law │  daughter   daughter    son
           │
        Rosita
     granddaughter
```

Pedro is ___Gloria's___ husband.

Pedro is _____, _____, and

_____ father.

Pedro is _____ grandfather.

Pedro is _____ father-in-law.

2 Give your teacher something you have with you, such as a notebook. Your teacher will put all the students' things in a bag and show them to the class one at a time. Whose is it? Guess. Follow the example.

Teacher: Whose is it?
Student: It's *Pedro's*.

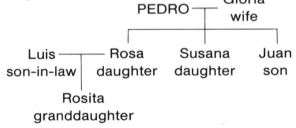

Focus on Vocabulary

Families

mother	grandmother	mother-in-law	aunt
father	grandfather	father-in-law	uncle
daughter	granddaughter	daughter-in-law	niece
son	grandson	son-in-law	nephew
sister	wife (or spouse)	sister-in-law	cousin
brother	husband (or spouse)	brother-in-law	

parents   children   sisters   brothers

 Connections: What does _____ mean?

Excuse me. What does niece mean?

A niece is your brother or sister's daughter.

Oh. Thanks.

Look at the words in the vocabulary box. Do you know all of them? Ask a classmate. Use the model above.

Focus on Vocabulary

Numbers

10	11	12	13	14	15	16	17	18	19	20
ten	eleven	twelve	thirteen	fourteen	fifteen	sixteen	seventeen	eighteen	nineteen	twenty

 3 Write the number you hear.

1. _____   3. _____

2. _____   4. _____

Alma
Pedro's
mother (65)

Gloria
Pedro's wife
(44)

PEDRO
(45)

Pablo
Maria's
husband
(42)

Maria
Pedro's
sister (40)

Alberto
Pedro's
brother (36)

Ana
Maria and
Pablo's
daughter (8)

Carlos
Maria and
Pablo's son
(13)

Luis
Gloria and
Pedro's
son-in-law
(25)

Rosa
Gloria and
Pedro's
daughter
(24)

Susana
Gloria and
Pedro's
daughter
(14)

Juan
Gloria and
Pedro's son
(22)

Rosita
Gloria and
Pedro's
granddaughter
(3 mo.)

4 **Work with a partner. Talk about the number of people in Pedro's family tree. Notice these special plural forms:**

man → men   child → children
woman → women   person → people

1. How many people are there?

2. How many adults are in the picture?

3. How many men are in the picture? How many women?

4. How many children are in the picture?

5. How many girls are in the picture? How many boys?

5 **Work with a partner. Together, write the names of the people in Pedro's family.**

1. wife _Gloria_   6. sister _____

2. daughters _____   7. brother _____

3. son _____   8. niece _____

4. son-in-law _____   9. nephew _____

5. grandchild _____   10. brother-in-law _____

6 **Fill in each blank with a word about family relationships.**

Luis is showing his wife Rosa's family tree to some friends from work

and is telling them about her family. "This is my _wife_____,

Rosa, and our baby _____, Rosita. These are Rosa's

parents. This is her _____, Gloria, and this is her

_____, Pedro. This is her _____, Juan, and

this is her _____, Susana. This is her _____,

her father's mother. This is her _____, Maria, and this is

her _____, Alberto. The others are her cousins.

Possessive Adjectives

Subject Pronouns		Possessive Adjectives	
I	am Pedro.	**My**	name is Pedro.
He	is my son, Juan.	**His**	name is Juan.
She	is my wife, Gloria.	**Her**	name is Gloria.
It	is Susana's bird, Lorenzo.	**Its**	name is Lorenzo.
We	are Rosita's grandparents.	**Our**	granddaughter's name is Rosita.
They	are our children.	**Their**	names are Rosa, Susana, and Juan.
You	have a nice family, Pedro.	**Your**	family is nice, Pedro.

Watch out for *his* and *her:*

Gloria's son
Her son

Pedro's daughter
His daughter

My, his, her, its, our, their, and *your* often tell who or what something belongs to. Use these words in front of a noun.

7 Tell about Pedro's family. Fill in the blanks with *his* or *her*.

Rosa is Pedro's daughter. Luis is ___*her*___ husband, and

Rosita is _____ daughter. Juan is _____

brother, and Susana is _____ sister. Pedro and Gloria are

_____ parents.

Luis is Pedro's son-in-law. Rosa is ___*his*___ wife. Gloria is

_____ mother-in-law. Susana is _____ sister-

in-law, and Juan is _____ brother-in-law. Rosita is

_____ daughter.

8 Write about Pedro's family. Use *my, your, his, her, its, our,* or *their*.

1. What is his wife's name?   _____ name is Gloria.

2. What is his son's name?   _____ name is Juan.

3. What are his daughters' names?   _____ names are Rosa and Susana.

4. What is his son-in-law's name?   _____ name is Luis.

5. What is his granddaughter's name? _____ name is Rosita.

6. What is the bird's name?   _____ name is Lorenzo.

Small Talk: Talking About Your Family

In the U.S. people often talk about their families when they meet for the first time. Single people usually talk about their parents, brothers, and sisters. Married people usually talk about their spouse and children.

In the U.S. it is usually not polite to ask adults these questions:

How old are you?

Why aren't you married?

Why don't you have children?

9   Practice the conversation.

Ewa: How many people are there in your family, Chan?

Chan: There are six people in my family. I have three sisters, one brother, and my mother. Tell me about your family.

Bring a photo of your family to class.

1. Your teacher will show the photos to the class and ask, *"Whose family is this?"* Can you guess whose families they are?

2. Work in groups of three or four. Tell your classmates about your family. Ask questions about each person's photo.

Possessives and Contractions

Who's = Who is	**Who's** that?
	That's my sister Mi-Cha.
Whose asks about possession.	**Whose** photo is that?
	That's Young-Soon's.
You're = You are	**You're** lucky.
Your describes possession.	**Your** family is nice.
It's = It is	**It's** Susana's bird.
Its describes possession.	**Its** name is Lorenzo.
They're = They are	**They're** my sister and brother-in-law.
Their describes possession.	**Their** baby is my nephew.

These words sound the same but are written differently because they have different meanings.

  10 **Read the conversation. Circle the right words. Compare your answers with a partner.**

Sumalee:	Is this **your** /**you're** family?
Young-Soon:	Yes, I live with my sister and her family.
Sumalee:	**Whose/Who's** this?
Young-Soon:	That's my sister Mi-Cha and that's my brother-in-law Jee. **Their/They're** very kind to me.
Sumalee:	They look like nice people. And **whose/who's** baby is this?
Young-Soon:	That's my nephew. He's **their/they're** son.
Sumalee:	He's really cute. What's that in his hand?
Young-Soon:	Oh, **its/it's** a rattle.
Sumalee:	**Your/You're** lucky to have such a nice family.

Focus on Vocabulary

Describing People

He has **curly** hair.
She has **straight** hair.

They are **tall** boys
They are **short** girls.

Adjectives do not have plural forms: They are talls girls.

11 **Listen. Your teacher will describe Chan's brother. Check (✓) the words that describe him.**

He is   ☐ tall
         ☐ short
         ☐ average height
         ☐ heavy
         ☐ thin
         ☐ average weight

His hair is   ☐ dark
            ☐ blond
            ☐ curly
            ☐ straight
            ☐ long
            ☐ short

He has   ☐ glasses
          ☐ a moustache
          ☐ a beard

He is   ☐ kind
        ☐ intelligent
        ☐ friendly
        ☐ helpful
        ☐ wise
        ☐ serious
        ☐ shy
        ☐ proud
        ☐ funny
        ☐ rich

12 **Work with a partner. Describe someone in your family photograph. Can your partner guess who it is?**

Example: *He is a tall man. He has curly hair.*

13 **Work with a partner. Describe someone in your class. Don't say the person's name. Who is it?**

In Your Own Words

Work in groups of three.

Get a large piece of paper and draw your family tree. Include your cousins, aunts, uncles, grandparents, in-laws, etc. Write one or more words like *tall*, *kind*, *funny* next to as many family members as you can.

Talk about your family. Ask each other, *"Who's this?"* Your group will then choose one family for someone to describe to the rest of the class. Use *his* or *her* as much as possible.

Example: *This is Teresa's family tree. This is her mother and this is her father. Her father is tall. . . .*

Wrapping Up

Complete the sentences with a word. Add *'s* to some of the words.

1. My father's sister is my ____*aunt*____.

2. My _____ or _____ son is my brother.

3. My uncle's son is my _____. My uncle's daughter is my _____, too.

4. My _____ husband is my son-in-law.

5. My son's son is my _____.

6. My husband's sister is my _____.

Can you solve this riddle?

My mother is your brother's mother. Who am I?

Write your own riddle.

Unit 8 Is the rice ready?

What do you see in the picture? What are they cooking?

Setting the Scene

Hue: Is the rice ready?
Carlos: Yes, it is.
Hue: Thanks, Carlos. Please chop two peppers.
Carlos: OK.

Count and Noncount Nouns

People think of *count nouns* as separate things. It is easy to count them.

1 pepper   2 peppers   3 peppers

People think of *noncount nouns* as wholes. It is *not* easy to count them.

rice

1 **Circle *count* or *noncount*.**

meat

count ~~noncount~~

mushrooms

count   noncount

tea

count   noncount

pea pods

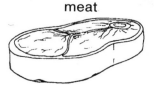

count   noncount

onions

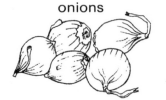

count   noncount

sugar

count   noncount

Count and Noncount Nouns (Agreement)

Count				Noncount		
There	**is**	**a green pepper** on the table.		There	**is**	beef on the table.
	are	**onions**		There's		beef on the table.
There's		a green pepper on the table.				

2 **What are the ingredients in Hanoi beef noodle soup? Work with a partner. Look at the picture. First, name the count and noncount nouns. Then, talk about what you see. Use *There's* or *There are* in the sentences.**

Example: A: There *are noodles* in the soup.
B: There's *beef* in the soup.

Some and Any

Count

Are there **any** onions?

    Yes, there are **some** onions.   No, there aren't **any** onions.

    Yes, there are **some**.   No, there aren't **any**.

    Yes, there are.   No, there aren't.

Noncount

Is there **any** rice?

    Yes, there is **some** rice.   No, there isn't **any** rice.

    Yes, there is **some**.   No, there isn't **any**.

    Yes, there is.   No, there isn't.

3 Work with a partner. Talk about what you see in the picture on page 75. Use the words below.

Example: A: *Are* there any *peppers*?

             B: Yes, there *are*. OR No, there *aren't*.

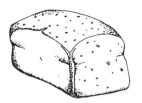

bread

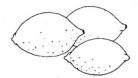

lemons

mushrooms

sugar

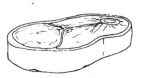

meat

pea pods

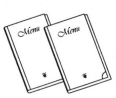

menus

rice

4 Hue orders food for the restaurant. Look at the refrigerator. Then look at his list. What does he need? Work with a partner. Check (✓) the things Hue needs.

Example: He needs *some* oil. He doesn't need *any* eggs.

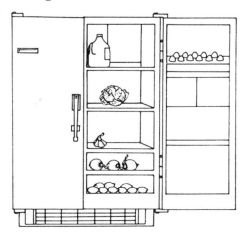

lemons		green beans
bread		chicken
eggs		lettuce
mushrooms		milk
garlic		hot peppers
onions	✓	oil

5 Which of the words in Exercise 4 are *count nouns*? Which are *noncount nouns*? Copy the words into the correct column.

Count   Noncount

_____ _____   _____ _____

_____ _____   _____ _____

_____ _____   _____ _____

_____ _____   _____ _____

6 Look around the classroom. What things do you think are *count nouns*? Which are *noncount nouns*? Write them below.

Count   Noncount

_____ _____   _____ _____

_____ _____   _____ _____

_____ _____   _____ _____

Commands

Commands tell people what to do.

Affirmative

Pay Here

Negative

DON'T WALK

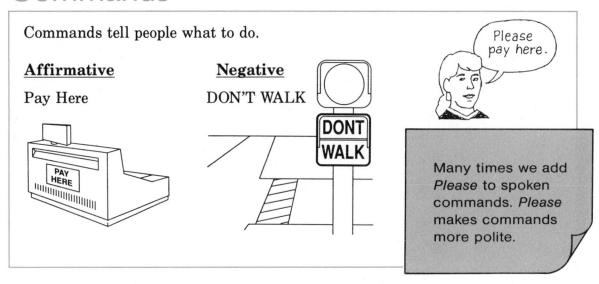

Please pay here.

Many times we add *Please* to spoken commands. *Please* makes commands more polite.

7 Find a partner. What do the signs say? Write the words in each picture. Use these phrases:

Push	Pick Up Prescriptions Here
Pull	Watch Your Step
Pay Here	Fragile: Handle with Care

Urgent Commands

Certain commands tell about danger.

Do not use *please* with warnings.

 8 **What should you say to the people in the pictures? There is more than one correct answer for each picture.**
Use these phrases:

Stop!	Don't do that!
Look out!	Don't touch that!
Watch out!	Be careful!

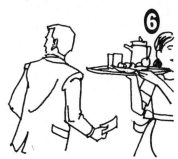

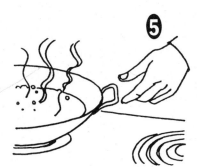

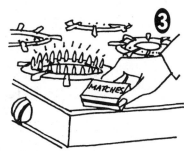

Use commands to give directions.

Turn right.

Turn left.

Go straight.

9 Work with a partner. Practice the conversation below. Then help Chan give directions from the other places. Use the words above and these phrases: *Go one block, Go two blocks, It's on the left*, and *It's on the right*.

1. Caller: I'm at the *bus station* now. How do I get to the restaurant?

    Chan: *Go straight* on Broad Street. *Turn right* on Main Street. The restaurant is *on the left*, next to the bank.

    Caller: I see. *Go straight. Turn right* on Main Street. It's next to the bank.

    Chan: That's right.

    Caller: Thank you very much.

    Chan: Sure.

2. The caller is at the library/ movie theater/train station.

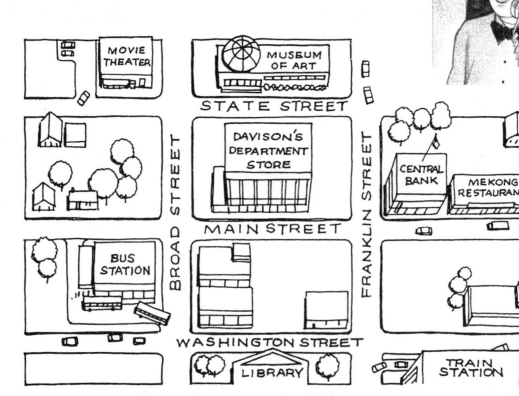

10 Work with a partner. Use the map on page 80. Give your partner directions to a place on the map. Begin at the school. Do not say the name of the place! Can your partner guess the place?

Give your partner directions to another place on the map.

In Your Own Words

Work with a partner. Tell your partner how to get somewhere from your English class.

Partnerwork ▶ Person A

Work with a partner. One person looks at the picture on this page only. The other person looks at the picture on page 82 only. There are six differences in the two pictures. What are they? Ask each other questions. Use the following model.

Example: A: *Are* there *any spring rolls* in your picture?
          B: Yes, there are some. OR No, there aren't any.

Work with a partner. One person looks at the picture on this page only. The other person looks at the picture on page 81 only. There are six differences in the two pictures. What are they? Ask each other questions. Use the following model.

Example: A: *Are there any spring rolls* in your picture?
B: Yes, there are some. OR No, there aren't any.

Wrapping Up

Work with a partner. Some customers left a mess at their table. First, talk about the mess. Use *There is* and *there are*. Then, tell Trang what to do. Use *pick up* and *clean up*.

Example: *There are some dirty plates on the table.* *Pick up the plates.*
There is some rice on the floor. *Clean up the floor.*

Unit 9   What's the weather like?

Talk about the picture. What do you see? What's the weather like?

Setting the Scene

"It's 32 degrees at
10 o'clock. It's
snowing now in Denver."

Introductory *It*

It introduces sentences about the weather, the temperature, and the time.

It's snowing now.   It's 32 degrees.   It's 10 o'clock.

The Appendix on page 174 lists the days and months.

It also introduces
days, months, and
years:

It's Monday.
It's October.
It's 1995.

1 **Work with a partner. Talk about the weather in each picture. Use the following sentences. Some pictures have two answers.**

It's snowing.   It's cold.   It's sunny.   It's windy.
It's raining.   It's hot.   It's cloudy.

 2 **Look outside the window. What's the weather like now? Is it windy? Is it raining?**

Small Talk: Talking About the Weather

In the United States, people talk about the weather a lot. They often say, "What a nice day!" or "What a terrible day!"

 3 **Work with a partner. Pretend you are waiting in line next to your partner. Talk about the weather. Use _very_ with words that end in _y_.**

Example: It's _very_ cloudy.

Focus on Vocabulary

Numbers

0	zero				
1	one	11	eleven		
2	two	12	twelve	30	thirty
3	three	13	thirteen	40	forty
4	four	14	fourteen	50	fifty
5	five	15	fifteen	60	sixty
6	six	16	sixteen	70	seventy
7	seven	17	seventeen	80	eighty
8	eight	18	eighteen	90	ninety
9	nine	19	nineteen	100	one hundred
10	ten	20	twenty		

This is the pattern for numbers 21 to 99:

21	twenty-one	26	twenty-six
22	twenty-two	27	twenty-seven
23	twenty-three	28	twenty-eight
24	twenty-four	29	twenty-nine
25	twenty-five	30	thirty

4 **Your teacher will read sentences about the temperature. Write down the number you hear.**

1. ___34___   2. _____   3. _____   4. _____

5. _____   6. _____   7. _____   8. _____

9. _____   10. _____   11. _____   12. _____

5 **Work in groups of three. Go around in a circle and count from 1 to 100. The first person says, "One," the second person says, "Two," and you keep going until you reach 100. Try not to forget any numbers!**

Listen carefully as your teacher says these numbers.

thirteen	thirty	seventeen	seventy
fourteen	forty	eighteen	eighty
fifteen	fifty	nineteen	ninety
sixteen	sixty		

6 **Circle the number you hear.**

1. (13) 30   2. 16 60   3. 19 90   4. 18 80

5. 17 70   6. 15 50   7. 14 40   8. 14 40

7 **Work with a partner. Say the pairs of numbers in Exercise 6. Take turns.**

Focus on Vocabulary

The Temperature
Most countries use the Celsius scale to talk about the temperature. The United States uses the Fahrenheit scale. Look at the thermometer. It shows the temperature in Fahrenheit and Celsius.

	Fahrenheit	**Celsius**
It's very hot.	100°	38°
It's hot.	85°	32°
It's warm.	70°	21°
It's mild.	60°	15°
It's cool.	50°	10°
It's chilly.	40°	4°
It's cold.	32°	0°
It's very cold.	20°	−6°
It's freezing!	0°	−18°

8 **Fill in the thermometers. Use any temperature you want. Then work with a partner. Ask for the temperatures on your partner's thermometers. What's the weather like? Is it cool? Is it warm?**

Example: A: *What's the weather like?*
           B: *It's 70°. It's warm.*

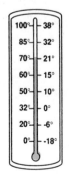 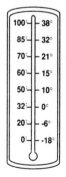 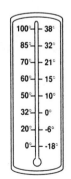 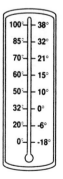

9 **What's the temperature outside today in Celsius? In Fahrenheit?**

Connections: What time is it?

What time is it?

It's one o'clock. It's six fifteen. It's nine thirty. It's two forty-five.

It's a quarter past six. It's half past nine. It's a quarter to three.

It's six ten. It's two fifty-five. It's noon. It's midnight.

It's ten past six. It's five to three.

A.M. starts at midnight and ends at 11:59 in the morning.

P.M. starts at noon and ends at 11:59 at night.

---

10 **Listen. Your teacher will read sentences about the time. Write down the times you hear.**

1. _6:30 P.M._   2. _____   3. _____   4. _____

5. _____   6. _____   7. _____   8. _____

9. _____   10. _____   11. _____   12. _____

11 **Work with a partner. Ask each other for the time. Say any time you want. Draw the time in the clocks.**

Clothing

a hat   T-shirts   scarves   a bathing suit

a sweater   a shirt   a skirt   a blouse

coats   a raincoat   jackets

a pair of boots   a pair of shoes   a pair of socks   a pair of shorts

a pair of pants   a pair of jeans   a pair of gloves   a pair of mittens

12 Tell the little girl what to wear. Match.

1. It's cool and cloudy.   Wear your raincoat and boots.

2. It's cold and it's snowing.   Wear your shorts and T-shirt.

3. It's warm and sunny.   Wear your bathing suit.

4. It's cool and it's raining.   Wear your coat, hat, and boots.

5. It's very hot and very sunny. You are going to the beach.   Wear your pants and jacket.

Present Continuous (An Introduction)

It **is snowing** in Denver now.

I'm	**not**	**wearing** a coat now.
You're		
He's		
She's		
(It's)		

We're	**not**	**wearing** coats now.
You're		
They're		

The present continuous describes actions that are happening right now.

> Remember to use both **be** (*am, are, is*) and the **-ing** form of the verb.
>
> It is snowing.

 13 Work with a partner. Talk about the pictures. What are Pedro, Ewa, Sumalee, and Abdul wearing? Is it hot, warm, cool, or cold?

 14 Work with a partner. Look at the pictures. The children are dressing to go outside. Each child forgot something. What aren't they wearing?

Example: *She's not wearing shoes.*

In Your Own Words

Think of a person in your class. Say a sentence about *one* thing that person is wearing. How many sentences can you make before somebody guesses who it is?

Example: *I'm thinking of a person. The person is wearing black socks.*

Partnerwork   ▶ Person A

Work with a partner. One person will be Person A. The other will be Person B. If you are Person A, look at this page only. If you are Person B, turn the page and look at page 92 only.

You work at a TV station in Houston, Texas, and you are preparing the weather map for a news program. But you are missing a lot of information!

Your partner works at a TV station in New York, New York. Your partner has the information you are missing. Ask your partner for the information you need.

Example: B: What's the weather like in *Houston*?
A: It's *70°*, and it's *warm*. It's *cloudy*.

Fill in the chart. Give your partner the information he or she asks for.

City	Temperature	Weather
Houston	70°F (warm)	cloudy
New York City		
Miami	84°F (hot)	sunny
Chicago		
Seattle	62°F (mild)	raining
San Francisco		

Work with a partner. One person will be Person A. The other will be Person B. If you are Person A, look at page 91 only. If you are Person B, look at this page only.

You work at a TV station in New York City and you are preparing the weather map for a news program. You are missing a lot of information!

Your partner works at a TV station in Houston, Texas. Your partner has the information you are missing. Ask your partner for the information you need. Don't look at your partner's chart!

Example: B: What's the weather like in *Houston*?
A: It's *70°*, and it's *warm*. It's *cloudy*.

Fill in the chart. Give your partner the information he or she asks for.

City	Temperature	Weather Activity
Houston	70° (warm)	warm and cloudy
New York City	33°F (cold)	snowing
Miami		
Chicago	40°F (cool)	cloudy and windy
Seattle		
San Francisco	68°F (mild)	foggy

Wrapping Up

What's the weather like today? What are people wearing? What are you wearing?

Think about the weather in your native country. What's the weather in your country like now? What are people wearing right now?

Review: Units 6–9

1 **Judy Harrison is from Chicago. Listen to your teacher read about Chicago. Then, read Judy's description of Chicago by yourself. Find these words. Are they count or noncount nouns?**

people	☐ count	☐ noncount	problems	☐ count	☐ noncount
buildings	☐ count	☐ noncount	traffic	☐ count	☐ noncount
opportunities	☐ count	☐ noncount	noise	☐ count	☐ noncount
businesses	☐ count	☐ noncount	pollution	☐ count	☐ noncount
factories	☐ count	☐ noncount	crime	☐ count	☐ noncount

Chicago is my hometown. It is a very large, busy city. There are people from all over the world here. There are many tall buildings, a subway system, and two main airports. There are opportunities for jobs and education because there are many businesses, stores, factories, and schools. There are many restaurants with food from many different countries. There are movies, plays, concerts, festivals, sporting events, and museums. It is an exciting city.

However, life is very busy in Chicago, and there are many problems too. There are many people and cars, so there is a lot of traffic and noise. The air is dirty because there is a lot of pollution. Also, many people are poor and there is a lot of crime.

2 **Work with a partner. Ask your partner about his or her hometown. Tell your partner about some of the good things about your hometown. Also talk about some of the bad things about your hometown. Make a list. Ask about the things listed in the exercise above. Other things you can talk about: Is there/Are there/a subway? museums? an airport? tall buildings? garbage? restaurants? farms? factories? churches? tourist attractions?**

Example: Let me tell you first about some of the good things in Chicago. In my hometown, there are job opportunities and good schools. There are people from many different countries.

Judy's Hometown: Chicago		
Good things about Chicago	Bad things about Chicago	
Job opportunities	traffic	
people from different countries	pollution	
	Cold weather in the winter	

3 Work in groups of three or four. Bring a book, pamphlet, or photograph to show the other students in your class some of the interesting places in your hometown.

If you do not have anything about your hometown, talk about a place in the United States instead. You can talk about a city you visited or a place in the city where you live now.

Example: This is a picture of downtown Chicago. This is the Art Institute. It is next to Grant Park.

4 Work with a partner. Talk about the weather in your hometown. Use these words:

snow	wind
rain	fog
sun	thunderstorms/showers

Example: Every season is different in Chicago. Fall is beautiful. It is cool and sunny then. Winter is very cold and windy. Sometimes there is a lot of snow. In spring, on some days it is very sunny and warm. It is rainy and cold on other days. In the summer it is hot and humid, but there are a lot of people outside then.

5 Pretend you are talking to your partner on the telephone. Your partner is now in his or her hometown. Ask your partner what the weather is like now. Tell him or her what the weather is like where you live now.

Example:
A: What's the weather like now in *Chicago*?
B: It's snowing right now. What's the weather like in *Mexico City*?
A: It's cloudy here.

◆ Present Continuous
   (Statements and Negative
   Statements)
◆ Present Continuous (Yes/No
   Questions and Short
   Answers)
◆ *Wh*-Question Formation

Unit 10 What are they doing?

What do you see in the picture? What are they doing?

Setting the Scene

Young-Soon:	That's my car! What are you doing?
Tow-truck driver:	I'm towing your car. This is a tow zone.

Present Continuous (Statements)

Young-Soon **is talking** to the tow-truck driver.

am	is	are
I | am talking	Young-Soon | is talking She He (It)	We | are talking They
I'm talking	**She's talking**	We're **They're talking**

Am, is, are + another verb with *-ing* can describe an action that is happening right now.

The Appendix on page 172 shows the spelling rules for the *-ing* form.

1 Work with a partner. Talk about the pictures. What are the people doing?

wait for the bus

buy ice cream

ride his bike

eat dinner

run to her car

read the newspaper

Present Continuous (Negative Statements)

Young-Soon is talking to the tow-truck driver. Now, he is not towing her car.

am	is	are
I **am not towing**	Young-Soon **is not towing** She He (It)	We **are not towing** They
I'm not towing	He**'s not towing**	We**'re** They**'re not towing**

Form negative statements in the present continuous by adding *not* between *am*, *is*, or *are* and the *-ing* form.

2 **Work with a partner. Look at the pictures below. Answer the questions.**

    Example: Read: *Is she driving* a car?
             Say: Yes, she is. OR
                    No, she*'s not driving* a car. She*'s riding a bicycle.*

1. Is she driving a car?   2. Is he taking the bus?   3. Are they reading?

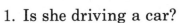

4. Is he drinking coffee?   5. Are they jogging?   6. Are they eating?

Neighborhood Places

auto repair shop	dry cleaners	movie theater	restaurant
bakery	health clinic	museum	shoe store
bank	gas station	park	_____
bus stop	grocery store	playground	_____
currency exchange	laundromat	police station	_____
department store	library	post office	_____

3 **Draw a line to complete each sentence. Then check your answers with a partner.**

1. Pedro is fixing the car at the   dry cleaners.

2. Sumalee is shopping at the   gas station.

3. Chan is choosing vegetables at the   laundromat.

4. Ewa is taking her dirty clothes to the   shoe store.

5. Anton is buying clothes at the   bakery.

6. Teresa is buying bread at the   auto repair shop.

7. Abdul is doing his laundry at the   grocery store.

8. Young-Soon is getting gas for the car at the   department store.

4 Fill in the blanks. Draw a line to complete each sentence. Then check your answers with a partner.

1. Fu *is depositing* (deposit) a check at the   movie theater.

2. Ewa ___ _____ (pay) bills at the   museum.

3. Anton ___ _____ (talk) to a nurse at the   playground.

4. Teresa ___ _____ (read) a book at the   post office.

5. Abdul ___ _____ (mail) a letter at the   bank.

6. Pedro ___ _____ (look) at an art exhibit at the   health clinic.

7. Chan ___ _____ (buy) popcorn at the   currency exchange.

8. Young-Soon ___ _____ (play) with her nephew at the   library.

5 Work in groups of three or four. Imagine you are at one of the places listed in the vocabulary box on page 98. Tell the people in your group what you are doing. Who can guess where you are? Follow the model. Take turns.

Example: A: I'm *reading a book.*
            B: Are you at the *park*?
            A: No, I'm not. *Other people are doing homework.*
            B: Are you at the *library*?
            A: Yes, I am.

Present Continuous (Yes/No Questions and Short Answers)

Is he **towing** my car?

He **is** **towing** Young-Soon's car. | Yes, he is.
Is he **towing** Young-Soon's car? | No, he's not.

They **are** **reading** at the park. | Yes, they are.
Are they **reading** at the park? | No, they're not.

Put the *am*, *is*, or *are* before the subject to make questions about actions that are happening now.

---

6 **Look at the picture. Listen to the question. Circle the correct short answer.**

1. Yes, they are.
   No, they're not.

2. Yes, she is.
   No, she's not.

3. Yes, it is.
   No, it's not.

4. Yes, he is.
   No, he's not.

5. Yes, they are.
   No, they're not.

6. Yes, he is.
   No, he's not.

7 **Work in groups of three. Each person writes down a sentence using the present continuous. Write each word of the sentence on a different card. Put a period** `.` **and a question mark** `?` **on a card, too.**

Example: HE IS BUYING BREAD AT THE BAKERY .

Mix up the cards. As a group, put the words in the correct order to make the sentences again. After you make the sentences, ask questions. Change the period `.` **to a question mark** `?` **.**

Wh-Question Formation

	Helping Verb	Subject	Main Verb	
What	is	Abdul	reading?	A book.
Where				At the library.

Most *wh*-questions need a helping verb, such as *am, is,* or *are,* before the subject.

> Questions about the person or thing that does the action (the subject) have different patterns.

8 What are the questions? Work with a partner. Ask and answer questions about these pictures.

1. Q: What's he doing?
   A: His laundry.

   Q: Where's he doing his laundry?
   A: At the laundromat.

2. Q:
   A: At the post office.

   Q:
   A: A package.

3. Q:
   A: Bread and pastries.

   Q:
   A: At the bakery.

4. Q:
   A: Her electric bill.

   Q:
   A: At the currency exchange.

Many Americans like to be busy. They like to talk about what they are doing. Here are some ways to talk about what people are doing:

What are you   working on?
                     studying?
                     fixing?
                     reading?
                     making?
                     cooking?

9   **Work with a partner. Practice the conversation. Make conversations about the pictures below.**

Example: Pedro: Hi, Teresa. What are you fixing?
                Teresa: An old stereo.

**Work in groups of three or four. Take turns. Pretend to do
something. Can the people in your group guess what it is? Use
only short answers.**

      Example: A: Are you drinking something hot?
                       B: Yes, I am.
                       C: Are you drinking coffee?
                       B: Yes, I am.

Here are some ideas:
**You are washing dishes. You are reading a very funny story. You are
talking on the telephone. You are watching a very sad movie.**

Partnerwork   ▶ Person A

**Work with a partner. One person looks at the picture on this page
only. The other person looks at the picture on page 104 only.
There are five differences in the two pictures. What are they? Ask
each other questions. Use the model.**

A: Is she buying a coat?
B: No, she's not.
A: What's she buying?
B: She's buying shoes.

Work with a partner. One person looks at the picture on this page only. The other person looks at the picture on the page 103 only. There are five differences in the two pictures. What are they? Ask each other questions. Use the model.

A: Is she buying a coat?
B: No, she's not.
A: What's she buying?
B: She's buying shoes.

Wrapping Up

Work with a partner. Look at the picture on page 100. Answer the questions. Use the model.

Example: Read: Are the two men playing baseball?
Say: They're not playing baseball. They're playing cards.

1. Are the two women on the left eating?
2. Is the boy talking to a friend?
3. Is the woman on the right writing?
4. Is the dog sleeping?
5. Is the man on the left drinking coffee?
6. Are the two men on the right reading?

Unit 11 Busy days

What do you see in the pictures? What is Ewa doing? What do you do every day?

Setting the Scene

Fu: So you work in a factory. What does your wife do?

Artur: She takes care of the children. And she sews neckties at home. Then she sells the neckties to a store.

Fu: Wow! You're both busy.

Simple Present (Statements)

I	sew	every day.	Ewa	sews	every day.
You		once a week.	She		once a week.
We		two times a week.	He		two times a week.
They					

Remember to add an -s to the verb with *he*, *she*, or *it*.

The simple present can describe things that happen again and again.

The Appendix on page 173 shows the spelling rules for *he*, *she*, and *it* with the simple present.

1 Work with a partner. Complete the sentences.

1. I ____sew____ neckties every day. (*sew*)

2. She _____ out the garbage every day. (*take*)

3. They _____ cans every month. (*recycle*)

4. We _____ to school every day. (*walk*)

Adverbs of Specific Frequency

How often does Ewa work?	every day/week/month/year.
	once a week.
Ewa sews ties	two times a week.
Ewa cleans the apartment	five times a week.
	on Tuesday/Thursday/Saturday.
	every morning/afternoon/evening.

The Appendix on page 174 lists the days of the week, the months of the year, and the seasons.

2 Listen to your teacher talk about Ewa's activities. When does she do these things? Check the days Ewa does each activity.

	Sun.	Mon.	Tues.	Wed.	Thurs.	Fri.	Sat.
1. Ewa prepares meals.	✓	✓	✓	✓	✓	✓	✓
2. Ewa takes care of the baby.							
3. Ewa cleans the apartment.							
4. Ewa does the laundry.							
5. Ewa buys groceries.							
6. Ewa takes the children to school.							
7. Ewa picks up the children at school.							
8. Ewa sews ties.							
9. Ewa goes to English class.							
10. Ewa plays basketball.							

3 Work with a partner. How often does Ewa do each activity in Exercise 2? Take out a piece of paper. Make a chart. Follow the model below.

Every day	Once a week	Two times a week	Five times a week
She prepares meals			

Housework

wash	dust	vacuum	sweep
dry	scrub	iron	fix things

Work with a partner. These pictures show things Ewa does every week. With your partner, match the words with the right picture.

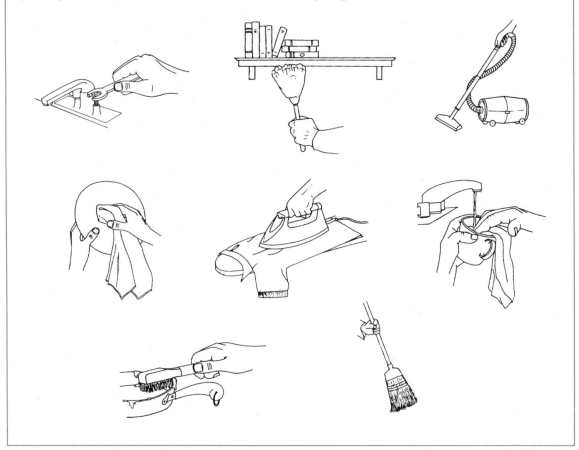

4 Work with a partner. Use the model.

Example: A: How often do you *iron clothes*?
B: *Once or twice a week.* How about you?
A: *Never!*

1. shop for food
2. iron clothes
3. change light bulbs
4. do the dishes
5. cook

6. do the laundry
7. fix things in your apartment
8. clean your apartment
9. recycle paper/cans/glass
10. take out the garbage

5 Work with a partner. This is what Ewa's husband, Artur, does each weekday. Talk about Artur's schedule.

Example: *He works at a furniture factory every day.*

Monday	Tuesday	Wednesday	Thursday	Friday
8:00 A.M.–6:00 P.M.	8:00 A.M.–6:00 P.M.	8:00 A.M.–6:00 P.M.	8:00 A.M.–6:00 P.M.	8:00 A.M.–6:00 P.M.
works at a furniture factory	works at a furniture factory	works at a furniture factory	works at a furniture factory	works at a furniture factory
6:30–9:00 P.M.	in the evening	6:30–9:00 P.M.	in the evening	7:00 P.M.–12:00 A.M.
takes English classes	takes care of the children	takes English classes	takes care of the children	delivers pizza

6 Write your weekly schedule on a piece of paper. Talk about your schedule with a partner. Follow the example below.

> Carmen's Schedule
> 11–3 I babysit for Jacob's family.
> 4–6 I go to English class.
> 7–11 I work at Superior Foods.

7 **Work with a partner. The Boksa family is busy. Talk about the things they do on Saturdays.**

1. What do they do in the morning? in the afternoon? in the evening?
2. Who works on Saturday? What do they do?
3. Who plays basketball on Saturday? When do they play?

In the morning

In the afternoon

In the evening

8 **Work with a partner. Talk about what you do on weekends.**

1. Do you work on weekends?
2. Do you go to English class on weekends?
3. Do you do housework on weekends?
4. Do you go to the park on weekends? to a restaurant? dancing?

Simple Present (Negative Statements)

I You We They	**do not** **don't**	
		work on Sundays.
Artur He She (It)	**does not** **doesn't**	

> In the negative, the main verb (work) does not change:
> He does not work.
> NOT
> He does not works.

Use the helping verb *do* or *does* to form negative sentences with the simple present.

9 **Listen to your teacher. Check (✓) the sentence you hear.**

1. ☐ Ewa works every day.
   ☐ Ewa doesn't work every day.

2. ☐ Artur works overtime.
   ☐ Artur doesn't work overtime.

3. ☐ They go grocery shopping together.
   ☐ They don't go grocery shopping together.

4. ☐ They go to the park together.
   ☐ They don't go to the park together.

10 **Work with a partner. The sentences below are wrong. Look at the family schedule on page 110 and correct them.**

Example: Read: Artur delivers pizza in the morning.
Say: *He doesn't deliver pizza in the morning. He delivers pizza in the afternoon.*

1. Artur delivers pizza in the morning.
2. Artur takes the children to the park in the evening.
3. Ewa goes shopping in the afternoon.
4. Ewa plays basketball in the evening.
5. Ewa's sister Monika works only in the morning.
6. Ewa's son Niki plays basketball in the afternoon.
7. Ewa's daughter, Rita, plays basketball in the afternoon.
8. The family relaxes together in the morning.

Focus on Vocabulary

Transportation

How do people travel?

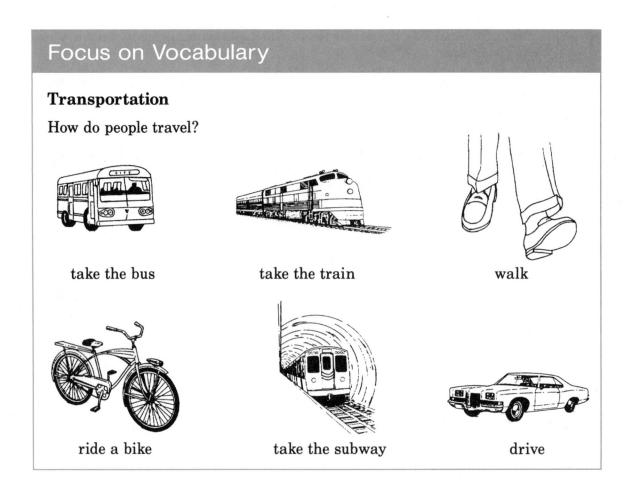

take the bus   take the train   walk

ride a bike   take the subway   drive

 11 **Work with a partner. Talk about how often you use each kind of transportation.**

      Example: A: How often do you *take the bus*?
                     B: Every day.

  12 **Work with a partner. Talk about the transportation you use. Complete the chart.**

      Example: A: How do you come to English class?
                     B: I take the bus.

	You	**Your Partner**
How do you come to English class?	car	bus
How do you go to work?		
How do you go grocery shopping?		
How do you visit your family?		
How do you visit your friends?		

13 **Work with a partner. Practice the conversation above. Use the train schedule below.**

Leave Evanston	Arrive Chicago	
5:50 A.M.	6:50 A.M.	**Fares:**
6:15	7:12	One-Way $ 2.75
7:30	8:30	Round-Trip $ 4.50
8:00	9:00	Monthly Pass $85.00
9:30	10:45	
11:30	12:35 P.M.	

1. It's 11:00. Ask for a one-way ticket.

2. It's 5:55. Ask for a round-trip ticket.

3. It's 9:10. Ask for a monthly pass.

4. It's 8:45. Ask for a one-way ticket.

Choose a partner. Answer each question in the box. Use expressions such as *every day, once a week,* and *never.* Then guess your partner's answers.

How many times did you guess the right answer?

Example: A: I think you get up before 7:00 every day.
B: Yes, I do. OR
No, only on *Mondays.* OR
No, never.

How often do you . . .	You	Your partner	
		Your guess	The truth
get up before 7:00?			
work on Saturday?			
take care of children?			
visit friends?			
study English?			
go to the park?			

Wrapping Up

Work with a partner. Talk about things you both do every day or every week. On a piece of paper, write two true sentences about things you both do. Then write one false sentence. Give your paper to someone else. That person reads the sentences aloud. Your classmates guess which sentence is false.

Example: Ewa and Pedro write:
1. We shop for food every week. (*True*)
2. We play basketball every week. (*False*)
3. We prepare meals every day. (*True*)

A classmate guesses:
Ewa and Pedro don't play basketball every week.
Ewa plays basketball every week.

Pedro doesn't play basketball every week.

Unit 12 Do you like to play soccer?

What do these people do on Sundays? What do you like to do in the park?

Setting the Scene

Sumalee:	Your team is great!
Abdul:	Thanks, Sumalee.
Sumalee:	Do you play soccer every Saturday?
Abdul:	Usually. Do you like to play soccer?
Sumalee:	Yes. A lot!
Abdul:	Great! Come next week.

Focus on Vocabulary

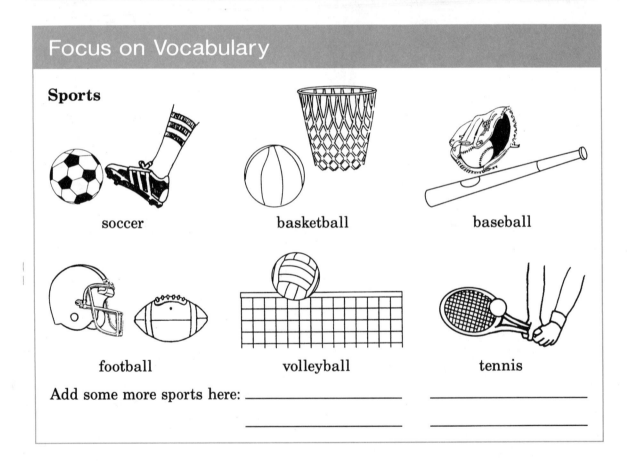

Sports

soccer   basketball   baseball

football   volleyball   tennis

Add some more sports here: _____   _____

_____   _____

1 Your teacher will read some sentences. Point to the sports word you hear in the vocabulary box above.

2 Find a partner. Talk about the sports you like. Do you have a favorite player or team?

Example: *I like basketball. My favorite team is the Chicago Bulls.*

Simple Present (Yes/No Questions and Short Answers)

Do	I you we they	play soccer?	Yes,	I you we they	do.	No,	I you we they	don't.
Does	he she	play soccer?	Yes,	he she	does.	No,	he she	doesn't.

Remember to form questions such as **Does** he **play** soccer? NOT Does he plays soccer?

The dog likes to swim. **Does it swim** every day?

Use *do* or *does* and the simple form of the verb to form questions in the simple present.

3 Look at the pictures. Listen to the question. Circle the right short answer.

1. Yes, she does.
   No, she doesn't.

2. Yes, she does.
   No, she doesn't.

3. Yes, they do.
   No, they don't.

4. Yes, we do.
   No, we don't.

5. Yes, it does.
   No, it doesn't.

6. Yes, I do.
   No, I don't.

4 Work in groups of three. Make nine cards. Each person gets three cards and writes a sport on each card. Put all the cards in a pile. Pick one card at a time and ask a question about it. Take turns. Answer truthfully!

Example: A: Do you play *soccer*?
         B: Yes, I do. OR No, I don't.

Leisure Activities

Which word does not belong in the list? Cross it out. Then check your answers with a partner.

1. listen to ~~books~~
   cassettes
   CDs
   music
   radios

2. watch movies
   music
   a soccer match
   TV
   videos

3. read books
   magazines
   newspapers
   videos

4. collect books of matches
   coins
   soccer matches
   stamps

5. play bingo
   cards
   chess
   newspapers

6. play the drums
   the guitar
   the piano
   the TV

5 Work with a partner. Talk about the pictures. What do they do on Sunday evening?

6 Work in groups of three. What do you do on Sunday evening?

Adverbs of Frequency

Do you **ever** play soccer?

| Yes, I | **always** **almost always** **usually** **often** **sometimes** | play soccer on Saturday. |
| No, I | **hardly ever** **never** | |

Words such as *always*, *sometimes*, and *never* tell how often something happens.

Put adverbs of frequency before most verbs.

7 Work with a partner. First, guess your partner's answers. Remember to add two of your own questions. Put a check (✓) in the column for your guess. Then ask your partner the questions. Mark your partner's real answers with a circle. How many times did you guess the right answer?

Do you ever . . .	always	almost always	usually	often	sometimes	hardly ever	never
1. play bingo on the weekend?				✓			○
2. exercise in the morning?							
3. play soccer in the evening?							
4. go to the movies on Thursday nights?							
5. listen to music at work?							
6. play cards at lunchtime?							
7.							
8.							

8 Work with a partner. Together put these words in the correct order. Write them on a piece of paper.

1. sometimes TV at watches Chan night

2. the Pedro sometimes in charango evening plays the

3. Young-Soon in usually jogging the goes morning

4. boxing never Ewa watches on matches TV

5. with Anton his usually at park on the children Sundays plays

6. walk Teresa in takes often evening the in a neighborhood her

9 Work in groups of three. Each person writes one sentence. Use the adverbs of frequency in the box on page 118. Write each word of the sentence on a different card. Write the period ⊡ on a card, too.

Example:

Abdul | usually | plays | soccer | in | the | park | on | Sunday | .
(10 cards)

Put all of the cards from all three people together and mix them up. As a group, put the words in the correct order to make the sentences again.

Information Questions (Simple Present)

	do	I you we they	**play** soccer?	At the park. On Sundays. Once a week.
Where When How often				
	does	he she (it)		

Use *do* or *does* and *play* (the base form of the verb) to form information questions in the simple present.

10 **What are they asking? Complete each question. Use *Where*, *When*, or *How often* and the words in parentheses.**

1. A: <u>How often do you play</u> soccer? (*you/play*)
   B: Once a week.

2. A: _____ ____ ____ ____ basketball? (*she/play*)
   B: At the gym.

3. A: _____ _____ _____ _____ volleyball? (*he/play*)
   B: On the weekends.

4. A: _____ _____ _____ _____ _____ to the beach? (*we/go*)
   B: A few times a year.

5. A: _____ _____ _____ _____ _____ to the park? (*they/go*)
   B: Once or twice a week.

6. A: _____ _____ _____ _____ on Saturdays? (*she/go*)
   B: To the gym.

11 **Talk to three classmates. Tell about your favorite place to go when you have free time. Ask, "Where do you like to go?" "When do you go there?" "How often do you go there?" Write your classmates' answers in the chart.**

Name of classmate	Where?	When?	How often?
Patricia	the movies	Saturday night	once a week

Like vs. *Like to*

Abdul	**likes**		soccer.
			(noun)
Young-Soon	**likes to**	**play**	soccer.
		(verb)	

Use ***like*** before a noun. Use ***like to*** before a verb.

Use *want* and *want to* and *need* and *need to* in the same way.

12 Part 1 Circle the correct form (*like* or *like to*) in each question below. Add two questions of your own.

	You	Your Partner
1. Do you (like) like to classical music?	yes	no
2. Do you like like to watch TV?	_____	_____
3. Do you like like to play cards?	_____	_____
4. Do you like like to football?	_____	_____
5. Do you like like to sew?	_____	_____
6. Do you like like to paint pictures?	_____	_____
7. Do you like like to visit museums?	_____	_____
8. Do you like like to books?	_____	_____
9. Do you like like to travel?	_____	_____
10. Do you like like to movies?	_____	_____
11. _____	_____	_____
12. _____	_____	_____

Part 2 Work with a partner. Ask each other the questions above. Write your answers and your partner's answers on the lines.

Example: Circle: Do you like (like to) play soccer?
        Say: A: Do you like to play soccer?
            B: Yes, a lot. OR
                 Yes, sometimes. OR
                 No, not much. OR
                 No, not at all.

13 Write the missing words in the blanks. Afterward, check your answers with a classmate. There is more than one right answer.

1. I like _____to_____ _____play_____ the guitar.

2. I like _____ _____ books.

3. I like _____ _____ TV.

4. I like _____ _____ to music.

5. I like _____ _____ museums.

6. I like _____ _____ cards.

7. I like _____ _____ to the radio.

8. I like _____ _____ at the beach.

14 Complete the following sentences on a piece of paper. All students give their papers to one person in the class. That person reads the papers aloud. Can you guess who wrote each one?

I like to go to _____

I like to play _____

I like to listen to _____

15 Work in groups of three or four. Find out what your partners like to do. How many things do all of you like to do? Find out as many things as possible that all of you like to do. Finish the sentences.

1. We like to listen to _____

2. We like to go to _____

3. We like to play _____

4. We like to watch _____

5. We don't like to go to _____

Add another sentence here: _____

_____

16 **Look at the chart below and add four activities of your own. Find someone in your class who likes to do one of the following things on the chart. Write that person's name on the line. Find a different person for each activity. Ask people who answer "yes" how often they do this activity.**

Example: A: Do you ever *play the guitar*?
          B: No, I don't. OR Yes, I do.
          A: How often do you *play the guitar*?
          B: Once or twice a week.

Add four more questions of your own.

Find someone who . . .	Name	How often?
1. plays the guitar	Mercedes	every day
2. plays soccer		
3. plays the guitar		
4. goes jogging		
5. rides a bicycle		
6. likes to play chess		
7. listens to rap music		
8. likes to watch horror films		
9. goes out to eat		
10. works overtime		
11.		
12.		
13.		
14.		

Work with a partner. Talk about what you like to do in your free time.

> What do you like to do in the park?
>
> I like to run and have picnics.
>
> Do you like to play soccer?
>
> Yes, a lot. Do you like to play soccer?

1. What do you like to do at home? cook? sew? fix your car? play with your children? take care of plants?

2. What games do you like to play? cards? chess? Monopoly? a game from your native country?

3. What kind of music do you like? rock 'n' roll? salsa? rap? jazz? reggae? classical music? music from your native country?

4. What kind of movies do you like? romances? horror movies? dramas? comedies? westerns?

Wrapping Up

Sumalee and Ewa are talking about what they like to do in their free time. Complete the conversation. Then work with a partner. Continue the conversation. Talk about yourselves.

Sumalee: What ___do___ you ___do___ (*do*) in your free time?

Ewa: Well, I _____ (*love*) music.

Sumalee: What kind of music _____ _____ _____ _____ _____ _____ (*like/listen to*)?

Ewa: I love jazz and blues. I _____ (*like*) Louis Armstrong and Billie Holliday.

Sumalee: _____ _____ _____ (*like*) Wynton Marsalis?

Ewa: Yes, _____ _____. I think he's great. How about you? What kind of music _____ _____ _____ (*like*)?

Review: Units 10–12

1 **Look at the pictures. The people are exercising or playing sports. Guess what they are doing. Write your questions on the lines. Then ask a partner your questions. Then your partner asks his or her questions. Who guessed the most correctly? Check your answers on the next page.**

Use these verbs:

dive	jump	play soccer	run or jog	swim
exercise	lift weights	play tennis	skate	walk

A: Are they walking?
B: Yes, they are. OR No, they're not.
     I think they're jogging.

1. _Are they walking?_   5. _____
2. _____ 6. _____
3. _____ 7. _____
4. _____ 8. _____

2 **Close your eyes. Listen to your teacher or a classmate do one of these actions: exercise, jump, run, walk. Can you guess which activity it is?**

3 **Work with a partner. Talk about which sports you like. Add three sports of your own at the bottom of the chart. Fill in the chart.**

Ask: Do you like to *ice skate*?

How often do you *ice skate*?

Some Possible Answers:
Yes, a lot.
Yes, a little.
No, not really.

Three times a week.
Two times a week.
Once a month.
Never.

	You		Your Partner	
	Like?	How often?	Like?	How often?
1. ice skate	yes	every winter	no	never
2. exercise				
3. jog				
4. play basketball				
5. play tennis				
6. roller skate				
7. run				
8. swim				
9. take a walk				
10.				
11.				
12.				

♦ *Can* of Ability: Statements
 and Negative Statements
   Yes/No Questions and
   Short Answers
    Pronunciation of *Can/Can't*
♦ Object Pronouns
♦ Present of *Have*
♦ *On, In, At* with Time

Unit 13 What's the matter?

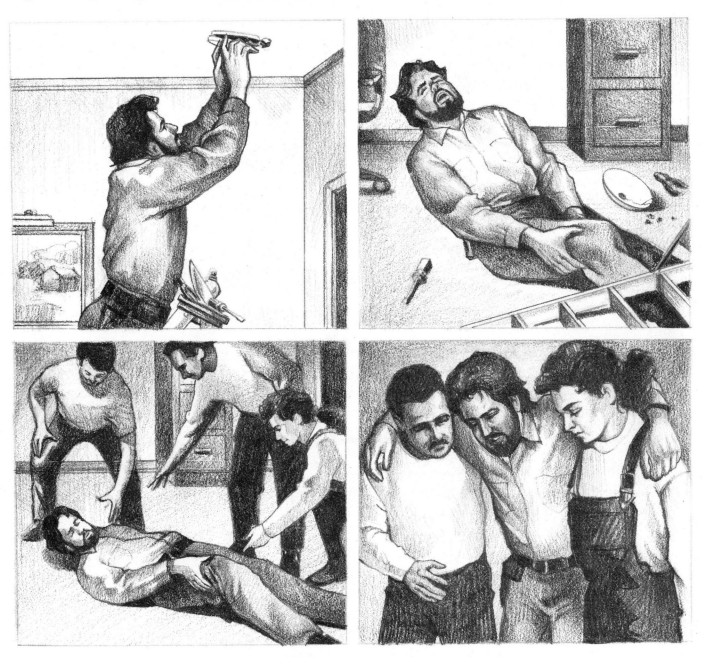

What do you see in the pictures? What is Anton doing? Can he move his leg?

Setting the Scene

Dr. Chin: What's the matter?
Anton: I hurt my leg.
Dr. Chin: Can you move it?
Anton: No, I can't. It hurts a lot.
Dr. Chin: Let's take an X-ray. I think you have a broken leg.

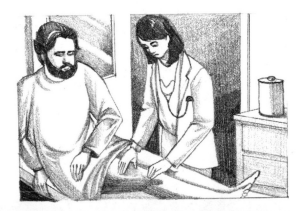

Can of Ability (Statements)

I		
You	**can**	work.
He		
She		
We		
They		

The dog is hurt. It **can** still walk.

We use *can* to talk about ability.

Can sometimes has other uses.

Can I leave now? (permission)

Can you help me? (request)

1 **Work with a partner. Anton needs to see the doctor three weeks from today. Look at the appointment book. When can the doctor see Anton?**

Time	Name	Time	Name
9:00	Thomas Udonov	10:30	
9:15		10:45	
9:30	Park Wang	11:00	Carmen Zamora
9:45		11:15	
10:00		11:30	
10:15	Susana Rodriguez	11:45	Peter Harris

Cannot (Negative Statements)

I	**cannot**	drive a car.
You		
He		
She	**can't**	
We		
They		

The dog is hurt. It **cannot** walk.

We use *cannot* to talk about inability.

Write *cannot* together as one word. *Can't* is the contraction.

2 **Work with a partner. Look at the pictures. Talk about the things Anton can and cannot do with a broken leg. Then, add some of your own ideas.**

Example: *He can't drive a car.*

Pronunciation of *Can/Can't*

English speakers say *can* very quickly.
Sometimes it is difficult to hear.

He can **WALK** now.

In a complete sentence, *can't* has a longer
vowel sound than *can*.

He **CAN'T** walk now.

3 **Listen. Your teacher will read some sentences. Can you hear the difference between *can* and *can't*? Check (✓) the sentence you hear.**

1. ☐ Tony can work long hours.
   ☐ Tony can't work long hours.

2. ☐ Susana can come to work early.
   ☐ Susana can't come to work early.

3. ☐ I can hear you clearly.
   ☐ I can't hear you clearly.

4. ☐ They can work overtime today.
   ☐ They can't work overtime today.

5. ☐ We can come Monday morning.
   ☐ We can't come Monday morning.

6. ☐ The doctor can see you today.
   ☐ The doctor can't see you today.

4 **Circle *can* or *can't* to make a true sentence about yourself. Then, work with a partner. Read your answers to your partner. When your partner reads his or her answers, listen for the difference between *can* and *can't*. Check the box for the word you hear.**

	can	can't
I can (can't) cook spaghetti sauce.	☐	☑
I can can't drive a car.	☐	☐
I can can't see well without glasses.	☐	☐
I can can't lift 100 pounds.	☐	☐
I can can't sew clothes.	☐	☐
I can can't go to my native country this year.	☐	☐

5 **Complete these sentences. Tell the truth. Then discuss your answers in groups of three.**

1. I can speak ＿＿＿＿＿＿＿＿＿, but I can't speak ＿＿＿＿＿＿＿＿＿.

2. I can play ＿＿＿＿＿＿＿＿＿, but I can't play ＿＿＿＿＿＿＿＿＿.

3. I can ＿＿＿＿＿＿＿＿＿, but I can't ＿＿＿＿＿＿＿＿＿.

Body Parts

Work with a partner. Together label the body parts in the picture.

head	eyes	neck	leg	wrist
chest	ears	shoulder	knee	thumb
hip	nose	arm	ankle	finger
~~back~~	mouth	elbow	foot	nail
hair	tongue	hand	toe	toenail

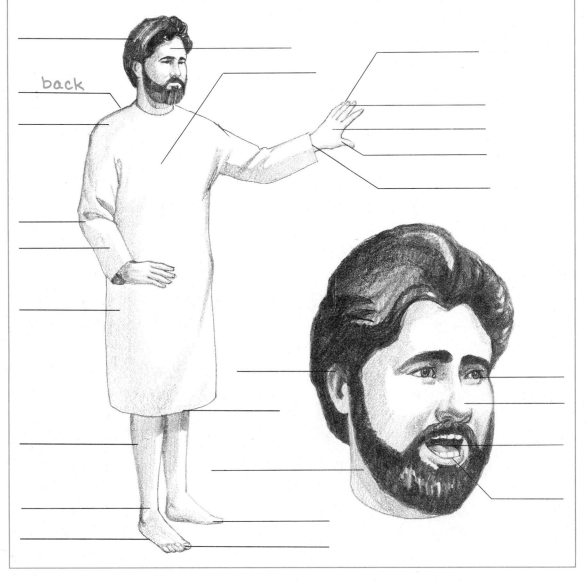

back

Can (Questions and Short Answers)

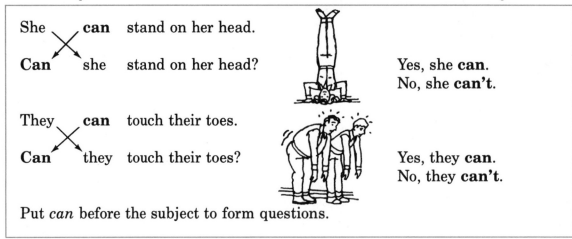

She \ **can** stand on her head.

Can / she stand on her head?

Yes, she **can**.
No, she **can't**.

They \ **can** touch their toes.

Can / they touch their toes?

Yes, they **can**.
No, they **can't**.

Put *can* before the subject to form questions.

6 Work in groups of three. Ask your partners if they can do the following things. Use this model.

Can you touch your toes?

No, I can't.

Yes, I can.

1. touch your toes
2. touch your ear with your elbow
3. touch your knee with your nose
4. touch your forehead with your knee
5. touch your nose with your tongue
6. wiggle your ears
7. stand on your head
8. put your elbows together

Object Pronouns

Subject Pronouns		Object Pronouns
I	⟶	me
you	⟶	you
he	⟶	him
she	⟶	her
it	⟶	it
we	⟶	us
they	⟶	them

Subject	Verb	Object
I	see	her.

7 **Your teacher will read some sentences. Write the object pronoun you hear.**

1. _____   5. _____
2. _____   6. _____
3. _____   7. _____
4. _____   8. _____

8 **What is the eye doctor asking? Complete each question. Follow the example. Then check your answers with a partner.**

1. Look at **the letter *E***.   Can you see _it_ ?
2. Look at **the boy**.   Can you see ___?
3. Look at **me**.   Can you see ___?
4. Look at **the woman**.   Can you see ___?
5. Look at **my finger**.   Can you see ___?
6. Look at **this letter**.   Can you see ___?
7. Look at **the nurse and me**.   Can you see ___?
8. Look at **these pictures**.   Can you see ___?

Present of *Have*

I You		a broken leg.	He She		
	have		It (the dog)	**has**	a broken leg.
We They		broken legs.			

We can use *have* to talk about a physical condition as well as possession.

9 **Fill in the blanks. Use *have* or *has*.**

The clinic is busy today. Many people want to see the doctor or the nurse. Many people _____ colds. Other people _____ young children who need checkups. A man _____ a broken leg. Another man _____ a bad backache. Some people _____ appointments, but others don't.

Aches and Pains

What does she have?   What do they have?

She has a **stomachache**.   They have **colds**.

a stomachache	a headache	a fever	a cut
a backache	a toothache	a cold	a burn

10 **Work with a partner. Look at the people. What do they have? Together, talk about the pictures. Use the words from the vocabulary box above. Label each picture.**

Example: *She has a stomachache.*

1. _a stomachache_ 2. _____ 3. _____ 4. _____

5. _____ 6. _____ 7. _____ 8. _____

11 **Work with a partner. Talk about the following pictures. How do the people feel? What do you think they have?**

Example: *He's sick. I think he has a cold.*

sick   dizzy   weak

On, In, and At with Time

	on	**in**	**at**
I have an appointment	on Monday	in the morning	at 7:00
She has an appointment	on a weekend	in the afternoon	at noon
	on March 13	in the evening	at night
	on Friday morning	in the winter	
		in January	
		in 1996	

On, *in*, and *at* with time expressions answer the question *When?*

12 **Listen. Your teacher will read some sentences. Write down the time expression.**

1. _on December 11_   5. _____

2. _____   6. _____

3. _____   7. _____

4. _____   8. _____

13 **Write *on*, *in*, or *at* for each of these time expressions. Can you do this exercise without looking at the vocabulary box above?**

1. _____ March 17   2. _____ the afternoon   3. _____ June 12

4. _____ the summer   5. _____ 1995   6. _____ night

7. _____ Tuesday   8. _____ 10:00 A.M.   9. _____ Sunday night

14 **Work in groups of three. Try to find a time when all of you can get together to review your English lessons. Then decide where you can get together.**

Example: A: Can we get together on Thursday evening?
                B: No, I can't. I work then.
                C: How about on Wednesday evening?

Work with a partner. One person will be Person A. The other person will be Person B. Person A wants to make an appointment at a clinic. Person B works at the clinic.

Before you begin, Person A writes *morning, afternoon,* or *evening* on a piece of paper. This is the only time Person A can go to the clinic. Person B writes four different times on a piece of paper. Those are the only times to make an appointment at the clinic.

Together, make a set of eight cards. Copy the words from the vocabulary box on page 134 (*fever, cold*). Person A will pick one of the cards and use the information in asking for an appointment.

Example: A: Hello. This is *Ewa Boksa.* My son is sick.
             B: What's the matter?
             A: *He has a bad stomachache.*
             B: Can you come *at 11:00 this morning*?
             A: No, we can't. We can only come *in the afternoon.*
             B: The doctor can see you *at 4:15.*
             A: OK.
             B: See you then.

Wrapping Up

On a piece of paper, write two things you can do well. Write two things you can't do well. Give your paper to your teacher. He or she will read each paper aloud. Can you guess who wrote each one?

- Past of *Be* (Statements and Negative Statements)
- Past of *Be* (Yes/No Questions and Short Answers)
- *At*, *On*, and *In* with Place
- Past Time Expressions

Unit 14 How much is this?

Where is Chan? What is he doing? What can you buy at this store?

Setting the Scene

Chan:	Excuse me, how much is that camera?
Saleswoman:	It's on sale now. It's $119.
Chan:	How much was it before?
Saleswoman:	It was $149.
Chan:	Can I see it, please?
Saleswoman:	Certainly.

Past of *Be* (Statements and Negative Statements)

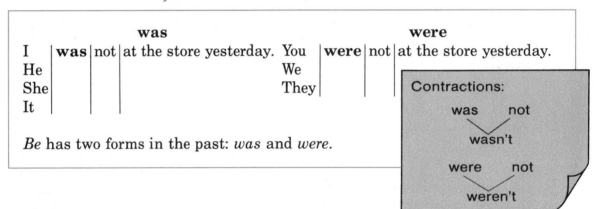

was

I / He / She / It | **was** | not | at the store yesterday.

were

You / We / They | **were** | not | at the store yesterday.

Be has two forms in the past: *was* and *were*.

Contractions:

was not → wasn't

were not → weren't

1   Work with a partner. Talk about the prices of the items below. What was the original price of each item? What is the sale price?

Example: *The Walkman is $12.99. It was $15.99.*

$15.99 $12.99

$29.99 $22.99

$24.99 $19.49

$6.99 $4.99

$19.99 $14.99

$12.99 $8.99

Money

Coins

| penny (cent) | nickel | dime | quarter | half-dollar |

 **Bills**

one dollar
a dollar bill

five dollars
a five-dollar bill

The word *money* is a noncount noun. The words *coins* and *bills* are count nouns.

2 Work with a partner. How much money is there?

3 Your teacher will show you a pile of money. Look at it for one minute. Then your teacher will make four changes. Look at the pile of money again. Talk about the changes with a partner.

Example: A: *I think there was one nickel before.*

B: *I think you're right. There were two five-dollar bills before. Now there's one ten-dollar bill.*

Repeat this activity in groups of two or three.

Past of *Be* (Yes/No Questions and Short Answers)

Was he at the mall yesterday?	Yes, he **was**. No, he **wasn't**.
Were they at the mall yesterday?	Yes, they **were**. No, they **weren't**.

4 Listen. Yesterday was a busy day at the mall. Look at the picture. Listen to the question. Circle the correct short answer.

Yes, she was.   Yes, she was.   Yes, they were.

No, she wasn't.   No, she wasn't.   No, they weren't.

5 Guess the conversation. Use questions and short answers with the past of *be*.

Teresa: _____Were_____ _____you_____ at home last night? I called you, but no one answered.

Chan: I _____ at the mall.

Teresa: Oh. _____ _____ crowded?

Chan: Yes, it _____. There _____ lots of people there.

Teresa: _____ lots of things on sale?

Chan: Some things _____ on sale, but most things _____ still expensive.

140   Unit 14

Focus on Vocabulary

Numbers

100	one hundred (a hundred)	1,000	one thousand (a thousand)
200	two hundred	10,000	ten thousand
300	three hundred	100,000	one hundred thousand
		1,000,000	one million (a million)

Written Form	Spoken Form
129	one hundred and twenty-nine
1,250	one thousand two hundred and fifty

6 **Your teacher will read some sentences about prices. Write down the price you hear.**

1. _$450.00_   2. _____   3. _____

4. _____   5. _____   6. _____

7. _____   8. _____   9. _____

7 **Write a sale price for each item in the picture. Then work with a partner. Talk about the original price and the sale price.**

Example: A: How much is that *Walkman*?
B: It's on sale for *twelve ninety-nine*.
A: How much was it before?
B: It was *fifteen ninety-nine*.

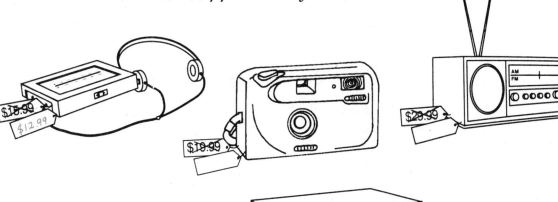

At, On, and *In* with Place

> **Where is the Sears Tower?**
>
> | | |
> |---|---|
> | It is **at** 233 South Wacker Drive **in** Chicago. | Use *at* with specific addresses. |
> | | Use *in* with names of buildings, cities, countries, or departments in buildings. |
> | **on** South Wacker Drive **on** the fourth floor | Use *on* with names of streets or specific floors of a building. |

8 Add *in, on,* or *at* to each of these phrases. Don't look at the box!

1. __*at*__ 101 Park Lane
2. _____ the seventh floor
3. _____ 612 South Elm Street
4. _____ Main Street
5. _____ the United States
6. _____ Los Angeles

Focus on Vocabulary

Places That Do Not Use *the*

I was	at	home.
You were	at	work.
		school.
		church/temple.

These places do not use *the* after *at.*

9 Write *the* in the blanks where it is necessary. Put an X in the other blanks.

1. at __X__ school
2. at _____ department store
3. at _____ home
4. at _____ temple
5. at _____ supermarket
6. at _____ park

10 Work with a partner. Answer the questions. Tell the truth.

Example: A: *Were you at the library last night?*
B: *No, I wasn't. I was at home.*

1. at the supermarket
2. at the mall
3. at the movies
4. at the park
5. at the library
6. at home
7. at the health clinic
8. at a friend's house
9. at work

Past Time Expressions

I was at the mall	yesterday.	a week ago.	last night.
	yesterday morning.	a month ago.	last Friday.
	yesterday afternoon.	two days ago.	last week.
	yesterday evening.	two years ago.	last weekend.
			last month.

Phrases such as *yesterday afternoon* tell when something happened in the past.

11 **Your teacher will tell you about what Anton did before his mother came to the United States. Write the time expression you hear.**

a year ago

_____ _____ _____ _____

12 **Work in groups of two or three. When was the last time you were at the following places? You also can say, "I never go there."**

Example: A: *When were you at the supermarket?*
B: *I was at the supermarket on Saturday.*

the supermarket	the library	the beach	a furniture store
a travel agency	the post office	the park	a clothing store
the airport	the consulate of your native country	the mall	an electronics store

Work with a partner. Practice these conversations. Then make up your own conversations. Use items that are in the classroom (a shirt, a sweater, an umbrella).

Customer:	I'd like to try on *this dress*.
Salesperson:	Certainly. The dressing room is over there.

Customer:	Do you have *these shoes* in *size 9*?
Salesperson:	Let me see if I have your size.

Salesperson:	Can I help you?
Customer:	Not now, thank you. I'm just looking.
Salesperson:	Let me know if I can help you with anything.

Customer:	Do you accept checks?
Clerk:	Yes. I need two forms of ID. We take credit cards too.

Ordinal Numbers

1st	2nd	3rd	4th	5th	6th	7th	8th	9th	10th
first	second	third	fourth	fifth	sixth	seventh	eighth	ninth	tenth

13 **Work with a partner. Practice this conversation. Use the department store directory below. Take turns being the salesperson and the customer. Add more items at the bottom of the page.**

Customer: Excuse me, where are *women's gloves*?

Salesperson: They're on the *lower level*, in the *women's accessories* department.

Customer: Thank you.

Store Directory	
Lower Level Women's Accessories Men's Accessories Cosmetics **First Floor** Juniors Young Men Young Women **Second Floor** Men's Clothing Shoes **Third Floor** Children's Clothing Children's Furnishings Toys	**Fourth Floor** Women's Clothing **Fifth Floor** Housewares Home Furnishings Bed and Bath Shop **Sixth Floor** Electronics Home Appliances Tools **Seventh Floor** Sporting Goods Cafeteria Customer Service

1. toys
2. sheets
3. perfumes
4. men's ties
5. men's sweaters
6. women's coats
7. children's shoes
8. baby cribs
9. pots and pans
10. toasters
11. clothes for teenagers
12. soccer balls
13. bicycles
14. _____
15. _____

Answer the questions about yourself. Tell the truth. Add two more places. Then talk to three people. Ask them the following questions. Write the answers in the chart.

When was the last time you were . . . ?				
1. at the supermarket				
2. on vacation				
3. in your native country				
4. on a plane				
5.				
6.				

In Your Own Words

Work in groups of three or four. Talk about a place you visted recently. Take turns asking each other about the place you visted.

Some questions to ask: When were you there?
Was it fun? interesting? boring?
Were the people there nice? friendly? helpful?
Was it expensive? cheap?

Wrapping Up

Complete the sentences.

1. I was _____ last night.

2. I was at the park _____.

3. I was at my friend _____'s house _____.

4. I was _____ last Saturday night.

◆ *A/An* and *Some*
◆ *A lot*, *Some*, and *Not any*
◆ *How much* and *How many*

Unit 15 How many do we need?

Abdul and Young-Soon are shopping for the class party. Where are they? What are they buying?

Setting the Scene

Abdul: How many onions do we need?

Young-Soon: A lot! Two pounds. How much parsley do we need?

Abdul: Just a little.

Young-Soon: OK. We need some peppers too.

A/An and Some

Count

| There's | a | pepper in the basket. |

| There are | some | onions. |

Noncount

| There's | some | parsley in the basket. |

Use *a* or *an* with a singular noun (one thing). Use *some* with plural nouns (more than one thing) and with noncount nouns.

1 **Work with a partner. First, look at the picture. What's on the table? Then draw some more food on the table. Talk about each other's pictures.**

Containers

Container words make it easy to count noncount nouns.

a **carton** of milk

two **bags** of rice

three **bottles** of oil

four **cans** of soup

Container words can be used with large amounts of count nouns too.

a **box** of raisins

two **jars** of olives

2 Work with a partner. One person looks at the picture on this page only. The other person looks at the picture on page 150 only. There are seven differences in the two pictures. What are they? Ask each other questions. Make a list of the items in each picture.

Example: A: Are there any bags of flour?
B: Yes. How many bags are in your picture?
A: There's one bag in my picture.

Work with a partner. One person looks at the picture on this page only. The other person looks at the picture on page 149 only. There are seven differences in the two pictures. What are they? Ask each other questions. Make a list of the items in each picture.

Example: A: Are there any bags of flour?
B: Yes. How many bags are in your picture?
A: There's one bag in my picture.

3 One word in each group is wrong. Cross it out. Then check your answers with a partner.

1. a box of   cereal
             crackers
             detergent
             ~~ketchup~~

2. a bag of   jelly
             flour
             nuts
             rice

3. a carton of   eggs
                 juice
                 milk
                 parsley

4. a jar of   instant coffee
            oil
            peanut butter
            mayonnaise

5. a bottle of   beer
              hot sauce
              soup
              ketchup

6. a can of   butter
            peas
            soup
            tuna fish

A lot, Some, and Not any

Count	Noncount
Count	**Noncount**
Are there any **carrots** in beef stew?	Is there any **salt** in beef stew?
 Yes, there are **a lot**.	 Yes, there's **a lot**.
Yes, there are **some**.	Yes, there's **some**.
No, there **aren't any**.	No, there **isn't any**.

4 Work with a partner. Talk about the picture. These are the ingredients for Abdul's Middle Eastern fava beans. One partner asks questions using the words in the list below. The other partner answers the questions.

Example: A: Are there any *beans*?
B: Yes, there are *a lot of beans*.

1. beans
2. potatoes
3. onions
4. garlic
5. lemon juice
6. oil
7. tomatoes
8. parsley
9. salt
10. pepper

5 Work in groups of three. Talk about the questions. Try to use *a lot, some,* and *not any*.

How much salt do you use in your food?

Do you drink coffee? Do you add milk or sugar? how much?

What do you eat or drink when you don't feel well?

Focus on Vocabulary

Measure Words

Measure words make it easy to count noncount nouns.

a half **gallon** of milk

one **tablespoon (T.)** of oil

two **teaspoons (t.)** of honey

three **cups (C.)** of water

We use measure words to talk about count nouns too.

one **pound** (lb.) of carrots   two **pounds** (lbs.) of carrots

The Appendix on page 174 lists weights and measures.

6 **Listen to your teacher read the ingredients for Teresa's guacamole. Complete each blank with the correct amount.**

_____2_____ avocados   _____ olive oil

_____ lemon juice   _____ chili pepper

_____ onion, chopped very finely   _____ salt

7 **What do you need to buy at the store right now? Make a list. How much of each item do you need? Tell a partner.**

Example: tomato sauce—one can
onions—two pounds

How much and *How many*

Noncount
How much milk   is there?

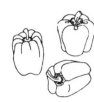

Count
How many peppers   are there?

How much is used with noncount nouns. *How many* is used with count nouns.

8 **Your teacher will tell you the ingredients for Anton's Russian meat pie. Circle the ingredients you hear. Check your answers with a partner.**

beef	oil	mushrooms	potatoes	sugar
onions	butter	parsley	peppers	garlic
sour cream	rice	tomatoes	salt	pepper

Then, on your own paper, write questions about the ingredients, such as "How much beef do you need for the pie?" Your teacher has the answers.

Partnerwork   ▶ Person A

Work with a partner. One of you will be Person A. The other will be Person B. Person A looks at this page only. Person B looks at page 154 only. Person A has the list of ingredients for New England Clam Chowder. Person B has the list of ingredients for Manhattan Clam Chowder. What are the differences? Make a list.

Example: A: Are there *clams* in your recipe?
            B: Yes, there are.
            A: *How many clams* are there?
            B: *One pint. How many clams are* there in your recipe?
            A: *One pint*, also.

<u>New England Clam Chowder</u>
1 pint clams, without shells   ½ cups water
2 tablespoons butter   1 teaspoon salt
2 cups potatoes, diced   ⅛ teaspoon pepper
1 onion, chopped finely   ⅛ teaspoon paprika
3 cups milk

Work with a partner. One of you will be Person A. The other will be Person B. Person A looks at page 153 only. Person B looks at this page only. Person A has the list of ingredients for New England Clam Chowder. Person B has the list of ingredients for Manhattan Clam Chowder. What are the differences? Make a list.

Example: A: Are there *clams* in your recipe?
  B: Yes, there *are*.
  A: *How many clams* are there?
  B: *One pint. How many clams are* there in your recipe?
  A: *One pint*, also.

Manhattan Clam Chowder
1 pint clams, without shells
1 onion, chopped finely
2 tablespoons butter
1½ cups carrots, diced
½ cup celery, diced
2 cups potatoes, diced

1 can tomatoes
  (28 ounce size)
1 tablespoon parsley,
  chopped finely
1½ teaspoon salt
⅛ teaspoon pepper

9 These are the directions for making a banana split. Put them in the correct order.

Put the cherry on top.

Add the chocolate sauce.

Put the whipped cream on top.

Split the banana in half.

Add the walnuts.

Add the ice cream.

Ways of Cooking Food

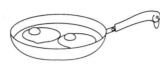
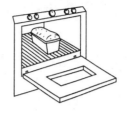

Check (✓) the ways you like to cook these foods. Add one more kind of food. Then work with a partner. Ask your partner about his or her answers. Do you have the same tastes?

Example: A: How do you like your eggs?
          B: I like to fry my eggs.
          A: I like to boil my eggs.

Food	Boil	Fry	Bake	Steam
eggs	✓			
beans				
fish				
potatoes				

10   Read about one way to make rice. Work with a partner and answer the questions.

Directions for Cooking Rice:

1. Put one cup of rice in a pot.
2. Add two cups of water.
3. Add one teaspoon of oil.
4. Bring to a boil.
5. Reduce heat, cover pot, and cook until water is absorbed. Makes three cups.

1. How much rice do you need?
2. How much water do you need?
3. How much oil do you need?
4. How much rice do you get?

Ask three classmates, "Do you make rice? How do you make rice?" Write the answers here. Start with one cup of uncooked rice.

Name	Water? How much?	What else?	Way of cooking?
Carmen	2 cups	onions, carrots, green peppers, oil, salt	boil

In Your Own Words

Work in groups of three. Tell about a favorite dish. What are the ingredients? How much of each ingredient do you use? Who cooks it? Can you prepare it?

Wrapping Up

Work with a partner. Talk about the picture. What is in the shopping basket?

Example: *There are some oranges.*
There is a large box of cereal.

Stop and Shop
Your One-Stop Supermarket

Stop and Shop Paper Napkins

SALE PRICE:
99¢
reg $1.39
100 count

Ultra White Detergent
SALE PRICE:

$2.⁹⁹ 2 lb. box
reg $3.89

Ground Beef
SALE PRICE:

$1.⁶⁹ per/lb.
reg. $2.19 per/lb.
Pure Premium

Chicken Legs
SALE PRICE:

69¢ per/lb.
reg. 99¢ per/lb.

Italian Sausage
SALE PRICE:

$1.⁹⁹ per/lb.
reg $2.69

Silky Shampoo
SALE PRICE:

$2.⁴⁹
15 oz. bottle   reg $3.19

Brite Toothpaste
SALE PRICE:
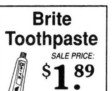
$1.⁸⁹
reg $2.59

Frozen Peas
SALE PRICE:
2 for

99¢
reg 79¢

Stop and Shop Ice Cream
Assorted varieties   SALE PRICE:

$1.⁹⁹
reg $2.79

Red Apples
SALE PRICE:

59¢ per/lb.
reg. 89¢ per/lb.

White Potatoes
SALE PRICE:

99¢ 10-lb. bag
reg $1.99

Spinach
SALE PRICE:

99¢ per/lb.
reg $1.49

Cabbage
SALE PRICE:

49¢ per/lb.
reg 69¢ per/lb.

1 **Work with a partner. Look at the ads on page 157. They show the sale items at Stop and Shop Market. Look at the chart below. Which things can Ewa buy on sale? How much were they (regular price)? How much are they now (sale price)?**

> **Example:** *Ewa can buy apples on sale. They were 89¢ a pound. Now they're 59¢ a pound.*

Which items can Ewa buy on sale?	Regular Price	Sale Price
apples	89¢ a lb.	59¢ a lb.

2 **Work with a partner. You have two dollars. What can you buy? How much can you buy?**

> **Example:** *I can buy Brite toothpaste.*
> *I can buy four pounds of cabbage.*

Teacher Script for Listening Exercises

Unit 1

Page 4
Exercise 5
1. e
2. d
3. n
4. j
5. b
6. s
7. o
8. v

Exercise 7
1. Davis, D-a-v-i-s
2. Miller, M-i-l-l-e-r
3. Wilson, W-i-l-s-o-n
4. Jones, J-o-n-e-s
5. Smith, S-m-i-t-h
6. Johnson, J-o-h-n-s-o-n

Unit 2

Page 11
Exercise 3
1. I am from India.
2. She's from El Salvador.
3. You're from the Philippines.
4. He is from Colombia.
5. They're from Somalia.
6. My friend's from Ethiopia.

Unit 3

Page 20
Exercise 1
1. Is Guatemala in Central America?
2. Thailand is in Southeast Asia.
3. Poland is next to Ukraine.
4. Is Egypt on the Mediterranean Sea?
5. Is Peru on the Pacific Ocean?
6. Is Uganda in Africa?

Page 21
Exercise 2
1. Are Teresa and her mother from Texas?
2. Is Sumalee from Russia?
3. Is Pedro from Peru?
4. Are Ewa and her husband from Thailand?
5. Is Abdul from Lebanon?
6. Is Anton from Russia?

Page 26
Exercise 10
1. 101 Main Street
2. 5523 Fullerton Avenue
3. 9782 Oak Street
4. 2437 Washington Street
5. Area code (213) 443-0910
6. Area code (616) 291-5654
7. Social security number 214-40-0239
8. Social security number 113-21-5798

Unit 4

Page 37
Exercise 5
1. daycare workers
2. nurses
3. student
4. cooks

Unit 6

Page 55
Exercise 4
1. Is there a cup on the table?
2. Is there a fork on the table?
3. Are there pans on the table?
4. Are there glasses on the table?
5. Are there dishes on the table?
6. Is there a pot on the stove?
7. Is there a blender in the cabinet?
8. Are there four chairs?

Page 56
Exercise 7
1. spoons
2. cabinet
3. tables
4. coffeemaker
5. dishes
6. glass
7. matches
8. knives

Page 60
Exercise 13
Read the paragraph for Exercise 14, on page 60.

Unit 7

Page 65
Exercise 3
1. 16
2. 13
3. 11
4. 18

Page 71
Exercise 11
Chan's brother is a kind man. He's average height, and he's thin. He has dark hair. His hair is short and straight. He has glasses. He is intelligent, helpful, and funny.

Unit 9

Page 86
Exercise 4
1. It's 34 degrees in Chicago.
2. It's 65 degrees in San Francisco.
3. It's 22 degrees in Anchorage.
4. It's 79 degrees in Miami.
5. It's 50 degrees in Washington, D.C.
6. It's 45 degrees in New York City.
7. It's 80 degrees in Dallas.
8. It's 0 degrees in Detroit.
9. It's 7 degrees in Dubuque.
10. It's 15 degrees in Minneapolis.
11. It's 91 degrees in Los Angeles.
12. It's 100 degrees in New Orleans.

Page 87
Exercise 6
1. 13
2. 16
3. 90
4. 18
5. 70
6. 15
7. 40
8. 14

Page 88
Exercise 10
1. He's eating dinner. It's 6:30 P.M.
2. She's leaving for work. It's 7:10 in the morning.
3. It's 8:15 P.M. We're starting our meeting.
4. It's 11:45 A.M. They're walking to the restaurant.
5. We're eating lunch. It's 12:00 P.M.
6. The baby's crying. It's 3:45 A.M.
7. I'm riding the train. It's 5:15 in the evening.
8. It's 6:50 in the morning. My alarm clock is ringing.
9. It's 7:40 A.M. I'm leaving the house.
10. We're watching the news. It's 10:20 at night.
11. It's midnight. He's doing the laundry.
12. They're drinking coffee. It's 3:25 in the afternoon.

Unit 10

Page 100
Exercise 6
1. Are the women on the left fighting?
2. Is the woman on the right reading?
3. Is the dog sleeping?
4. Is the man on the left eating?
5. Are the men on the right singing?
6. Is the boy listening to the radio?

Unit 11

Page 107
Exercise 2
1. Ewa prepares meals every day.
2. Ewa takes care of the baby every day.
3. Ewa cleans the apartment on Tuesday and Thursday.
4. Ewa does the laundry on Monday.
5. Ewa buys groceries on Tuesday and Friday.
6. Ewa takes the children to school Monday through Friday.
7. Ewa picks up the children at school Monday through Friday.
8. Ewa sews ties on Monday, Wednesday, Friday, and Saturday.
9. Ewa goes to English class on Tuesday and Thursday evenings.
10. Ewa plays basketball on Saturday.

Page 111
Exercise 9
1. Ewa works every day.
2. Artur doesn't work overtime.
3. They don't go grocery shopping together.
4. They go to the park together.

Unit 12

Page 116
Exercise 1
1. Abdul likes to play **soccer** on weekends.
2. Young-Soon plays **tennis** on Saturday.
3. Anton likes to watch **football** games.
4. Chan plays **baseball** a lot.
5. Teresa often goes to **basketball** games.
6. Ewa likes to play **volleyball** in the summer.

Page 117
Exercise 3
1. Does she play **tennis** with her friends?
2. Does she play **basketball** after work?
3. Do they **lift weights** at the gym?
4. Do we **do exercises** together?
5. Does it **play Frisbee**?
6. Do I **dive** at the pool?

Unit 13

Page 130
Exercise 3
1. Tony can work long hours.
2. Susana can't come to work early.
3. I can't hear you clearly.
4. They can work overtime today.
5. We can come Monday morning.
6. The doctor can't see you today.

Page 133
Exercise 7
1. I see her. She's next to the door.
2. I hear him. He's talking to the nurse.
3. I hear them. They're talking in the hall.
4. I see it. The appointment book is on the floor.
5. I am listening to it. The radio's playing.
6. I can't see her. She's in the waiting room.
7. I can't talk to him. His line is busy.
8. I can't find them. I think they're in the hall.

Page 135
Exercise 12
1. Your appointment is on December 11.
2. The doctor is here on Tuesday morning.
3. They had chicken pox in 1968.
4. We take vitamin C in the winter.
5. Many nurses work at night.
6. Call the clinic at 3:15.
7. The receptionist eats lunch at noon.
8. August 14 is your next appointment. See you in August.

Unit 14

Page 140
Exercise 4
1. Was she at the supermarket?
2. Was she tired?
3. Were the earrings cheap?

Page 141
Exercise 6
Last year, prices were different from what they are now.

1. Two airplane tickets from New York City to Mexico City were $450.
2. A small TV was $149.
3. A small sofa was $345.
4. A camera was $129.
5. A three-bedroom house was $129,000.
6. A new economy car was $3,950.
7. A new luxury car was $28,599.
8. A new luxury boat was $500,000.
9. A fabulous mansion was $1,250,000.

Page 143
Exercise 11
Anton's mother is moving to the United States. She is going to live with Anton and his family. Anton is very excited. **A year ago**, he went to the Russian Consulate to get the right papers for her to leave Russia. **Last March**, he went to the Immigration and Naturalization Service to get information about immigration. **Last month**, he also went to a travel agency to buy an airplane ticket for his mother. **Last Saturday**, he went to a resale store to buy a bed for his mother. **Yesterday morning**, he went to the grocery store to buy her favorite food. **This morning**, he took the bus to the airport. **This afternoon**, he met his mother. He was very happy. **Now**, they are at home, talking and eating. They are very happy.

Unit 15

Page 152
Exercise 6
1. Two avocados
2. Three tablespoons of lemon juice
3. One tablespoon onion, chopped very finely
4. One teaspoon olive oil
5. One chili pepper
6. ½ teaspoon salt

Page 153
Exercise 8
Two onions
Two tablespoons butter
½ pound mushrooms
¾ pound beef
1 teaspoon salt
⅛ teaspoon pepper
½ cup sour cream

Appendix

Page 169
Exercise 2
1. class
2. pencil
3. paper
4. eraser
5. name
6. computer

Page 170
Exercise 1
1. glasses
2. spoons
3. boxes
4. names
5. papers
6. matches
7. hoses
8. prices
9. students

Appendix

Some Popular Names in the United States

First Names (Male)

Aaron
Adam
Alan, Allen
Alexander (Alex)
Andrew (Andy)
Anthony
Benjamin (Ben)
Brian, Bryan
Carl
Charles (Charlie, Chuck)
Christopher (Chris)
Craig
Daniel (Dan, Danny)
David (Dave)
Dennis
Derek (Derrick)
Donald (Don)
Douglas (Doug)
Edward (Ed)
Eric, Erik
Frank

Gabriel (Gabe)
Gary
George
Gregory (Greg)
Harold (Harry)
Henry (Hank)
James (Jim, Jimmy, Jamie, Jay)
Jason
Jeffrey, Geoffrey (Jeff)
Jeremy
Jesse
John (Johnny)
Jonathan (Jon)
Joseph (Joe)
Keith
Kenneth (Ken)
Kevin
Lawrence (Larry)
Mark, Marcus
Matthew (Matt)
Michael (Mike)

Nicholas (Nick)
Patrick (Pat)
Paul
Peter (Pete)
Phillip, Philip (Phil)
Richard (Dick, Rich, Rick)
Robert (Bob, Bobby, Rob)
Ronald (Ron)
Samuel (Sam)
Scott
Sean, Shawn
Stephen, Steven (Steve)
Thomas (Tom, Tommy)
Timothy (Tim)
Vincent (Vince)
William (Bill, Billy Willie)
Zachary (Zach)

First Names (Female)

Alexandra
Alicia, Alice
Allison
Amanda
Amy
Angela
Anna, Ann, Anne
Bonnie
Carolyn, Caroline (Carol, Carrie)
Catherine, Katherine, Kathryn (Cathy, Kathy, Kate, Katie)
Christine, Christina (Chris)
Cynthia (Cindy, Cindi)
Dawn
Deborah (Debbie)
Dorothy
Elizabeth (Beth, Betsy, Betty, Liz)
Emily
Erica
Frances (Fran)

Gina
Helen
Jacqueline (Jackie)
Jamie
Jane, Jean
Jennifer (Jenny)
Jessica (Jessie)
Julie, Julia
Karen
Kate, Katie
Kelly
Kimberly (Kim)
Kristen, Kristin (Kris)
Laura, Lauren
Leslie
Lisa
Louise
Margaret (Peggy)
Marie, Maria
Mary

Melinda (Linda)
Melissa
Michelle
Molly
Nancy
Natalie
Nicole
Pamela (Pam)
Rachel
Rebecca (Becky)
Ruth
Sara, Sarah
Stacy, Stacey
Stephanie
Susan (Sue, Susie)
Tanya
Tiffany
Tina
Vanessa
Victoria

Last Names

The ten most common last names in the United States are:

Anderson	Martin
Brown	Miller
Davis	Smith
Johnson	Williams
Jones	Wilson

Other common American last names are:

Adams	Harris	Rodríguez
Allen	Hill	Ross
Bell	Howard	Sánchez
Campbell	Jackson	Scott
Carter	James	Sullivan
Clark	Kelly, Kelley	Taylor
Coleman	Kim	Thomas
Collins	King	Thompson
Evans	Lewis	Turner
Goodman	Martin	Walker
Goldberg	Mitchell	Wang
González	Moore	Washington
Gordon	Morris	White
Green, Greene	Murphy	Wright
Griffin	Nelson	Young
Hall	Peterson	
	Robinson	

Sources

Bingwanger, Barbara, and Lisbeth Mah. *The Best Name for Your Baby.* New York: Henry, Holt and Company, 1990.

Dunkling, Leslie, and William Gosling. *The New American Dictionary of Baby Names.* New York: Signet, 1983.

Lansky, Bruce. *The Best Baby Name Book in the Whole Wide World.* New York: Meadowbrook, Inc., 1984.

United States Social Security Administration

Countries and Nationalities

Afghanistan	Afghani	Egypt	Egyptian
Albania	Albanian	El Salvador	Salvadoran
Algeria	Algerian	Equatorial Guinea	Equitorial Guinean
Andorra	Andorran	Estonia	Estonian
Angola	Angolan	Ethiopia	Ethiopian
Antigua and Barbuda	Antiguan	Fiji	Fijian
Argentina	Argentine	Finland	Finnish
Armenia	Armenian	France	French
Australia	Australian	Gabon	Gabonese
Austria	Austrian	Gambia	Gambian
Azerbaijan	Azerbaijani	Georgia	Georgian
Bahamas	Bahamian	Germany	German
Bahrain	Bahraini	Ghana	Ghanaian
Bangladesh	Bangladesh	Greece	Greek
Barbados	Barbadian	Grenada	Grenadian
Belarus	Belorussian	Guatemala	Guatemalan
Belgium	Belgian	Guinea	Guinean
Belize	Belizean	Guinea-Bissau	Guinea-Bissauan
Benin	Beninese	Guyana	Guyanese
Bhutan	Bhutanese	Haiti	Haitian
Bolivia	Bolivian	Honduras	Honduran
Botswana	Batswana	Hungary	Hungarian
Brazil	Brazilian	Iceland	Icelandic
Brunei	Bruneian	India	Indian
Bulgaria	Bulgarian	Indonesia	Indonesian
Burkina Faso	Burkinabe	Iran	Iranian
Burundi	Burundian	Iraq	Iraqi
Cambodia	Cambodian	Ireland	Irish
Cameroon	Cameroonian	Israel	Israeli
Canada	Canadian	Italy	Italian
Cape Verde	Cape Verdian	Ivory Coast	Ivorian
Central African Republic	Central African	Jamaica	Jamaican
		Japan	Japanese
Chad	Chadian	Jordan	Jordanian
Chile	Chilean	Kazakhstan	Kazakh
China	Chinese	Kenya	Kenyan
Colombia	Colombian	Kuwait	Kuwaiti
Comoros	Comoran	Kyrgyzstan	Kyrgyz
Congo	Congolese	Laos	Laotian
Costa Rica	Costa Rican	Latvia	Latvian
Cuba	Cuban	Lebanon	Lebanese
Cyprus	Cypriot	Lesotho	Basotho
Czech Republic	Czech	Liberia	Liberian
Denmark	Danish	Libya	Libyan
Djibouti	Djiboutian	Liechtenstein	Liechtensteiner
Dominica	Dominican	Lithuania	Lithuanian
Dominican Republic	Dominican	Luxembourg	Luxembourger
Ecuador	Ecuadorian	Madagascar	Madagascan

Malawi	Malawian	Solomon Islands	Solomon Islander
Malaysia	Malaysian	Somalia	Somali
Maldives	Maldivian	South Africa	South African
Mali	Malian	South Korea	Korean
Malta	Maltese	Spain	Spanish
Mauritania	Mauritanian	Sri Lanka	Sri Lankan
Mauritius	Mauritian	Sudan	Sudanese
Mexico	Mexican	Suriname	Surinamese
Moldova	Moldovan	Swaziland	Swazi
Mongolia	Mongolian	Sweden	Swedish
Morocco	Moroccan	Switzerland	Swiss
Mozambique	Mozambican	Syria	Syrian
Namibia	Namibian	Taiwan	Taiwanese
Nepal	Nepalese	Tajikstan	Tajik
The Netherlands	Dutch	Thailand	Thai
New Zealand	New Zealander	Togo	Togolese
Nicaragua	Nicaraguan	Trinidad and	Trinidadian,
Niger	Nigerien	Tobago	Tobagonian
Nigeria	Nigerian	Tunisia	Tunisian
North Korea	Korean	Turkey	Turkish/Turk
Norway	Norwegian	Turkmenistan	Turkmen
Oman	Omani	Uganda	Ugandan
Pakistan	Pakistani	Ukraine	Ukrainian
Panama	Panamanian	United Arab Emirates	Emirian
Papua New Guinea	Papua New Guinean	United Kingdom	British
		United States	American
Paraguay	Paraguayan	Uruguay	Uruguayan
Peru	Peruvian	Uzbekistan	Uzbek
Philippines	Filipino	Vanuatu	Vanuatuan
Poland	Polish	Venezuela	Venezuelan
Portugal	Portugese	Vietnam	Vietnamese
Qatar	Qatari	Yemen	Yemeni
Romania	Romanian	Zaire	Zairian
Russia	Russian	Zambia	Zambian
Rwanda	Rwandan	Zimbabwe	Zimbabwean
Saint Kitts Nevis	Kittsian, Nevisian		
Saint Lucia	Saint Lucian		
Saint Vincent and the Grenadines	Saint Vincentian	**Also:**	
		Palestine	Palestinian
Samoa	Samoan	Puerto Rico	Puerto Rican
Sao Tome and Principe	Sao Tomean	Scotland	Scots (Scottish)
		Wales	Welsh
Saudi Arabia	Saudi (Arabian)	_____	_____
Senegal	Senegalese		
Seychelles	Seychellois	_____	_____
Sierra Leone	Sierra Leonean	_____	_____
Singapore	Singaporean		
Slovakia	Slovak	_____	_____

World Map

Greenland

Iceland

United Kingdom

Ireland

Netherlands

Belgium

Luxembourg

Switzerland

Austria

Portugal

Canada

NORTH AMERICA

United States of America

ATLANTIC OCEAN

Morocco

Algeria

Western Sahara

Mexico

Bahamas

Cuba

Dominican Republic

Puerto Rico

Jamaica

Belize

Haiti

Mauritania

Mali

Senegal

Guatemala

Honduras

Dominica

The Gambia

Burkina Faso

El Salvador

Nicaragua

Barbados

Guinea-Bissau

Guinea

Costa Rica

Panama

Trinidad and Tobago

Venezuela

Guyana

Sierra Leone

Liberia

Colombia

Suriname

Ivory Coast

Equato

Ecuador

French Guiana

Ghana

Gui

Togo

Peru

SOUTH AMERICA

Benin

Sao Tome and Principe

Brazil

Bolivia

Paraguay

Chile

Uruguay

Argentina

C OCEAN

Russia

Estonia
Latvia
Lithuania
Poland
Belarus
zech Republic   Kazakhstan

Bosnia and Herzegovina
Geo

n Korea   Japan

Taiwan   PACIFIC OCEAN

United
Arab Emirates
Oman

nam
aos
dia   Philippines

Djibouti

alia   Sri Lanka

Central   INDIAN OCEAN   Brunei
rican Republic   alaysia
Maldives   ingapore

FRICA

Zaire

da
undi   Seychelles

Comoros   Indonesia   Solomon Islands

o   Papua New Guinea

Madagascar
e
Mauritius

Mozambique
Swaziland   Australia

Lesotho
ca

New Zealand

ANTARCTICA

Teresa is single.

Olga Robles is married.

Judy Harrison is married.

Use *Ms.* or *Miss*, but she likes *Ms.* better.

Use *Ms.* or *Mrs.*, but she likes *Mrs.* better.

Use *Ms.* or *Mrs.*, but she likes *Ms.* better.

Ms. Teresa Ortega

Mrs. Olga Robles

Ms. Judy Harrison

Use a title with a person's first and last name or with a person's last name only.

Example: Ms. Judy Harrison
Ms. Harrison

~~Ms. Judy~~

Mr.   is used for any man.

Ms.   is used for any woman—single, married, widowed, or divorced. It is the best title to use for business or when you do not know if someone is married or single.

Miss   is used for women who are single.

Mrs.   is used for women who are now married, widowed, or divorced.

Some people do not like to use titles. They use their first and last names only.

Syllables

Listen to your teacher say the following words. Some of the words have more than one syllable or part.

1 syllable   2 syllables   3 syllables

$\frac{\text{dish}}{1}$ $\frac{\text{dish}}{1}\frac{\text{es}}{2}$ (dishes) $\frac{\text{dish}}{1}\frac{\text{wash}}{2}\frac{\text{er}}{3}$ (dishwasher)

1 **Your teacher will read the following words. Tap on your desk one time for each syllable that you hear.**

   1. rice   2. fork   3. spoon   4. chair

   5. toaster   6. glasses   7. boxes   8. oven

2 **Your teacher will read some words. Write them down. Then write the number of syllables next to each word.**

   1. _____ ___   2. _____ ___   3. _____ ___

   4. _____ ___   5. _____ ___   6. _____ ___

3 **How many syllables are in your name? Write each syllable below. Add more lines if you need them.**

   Example: First Name: $\frac{\text{Dan}}{1}$ Last Name: $\frac{\text{So}}{1}\frac{\text{to}}{2}\frac{\text{ma}}{3}\frac{\text{yor}}{4}$

   _____ _____ _____ _____ _____ _____
     1   2   3   4   5   6

   Last Name

   _____ _____ _____ _____ _____ _____
     1   2   3   4   5   6

4 **Work with a partner. Say your first and last name. Your partner will tap on the desk the number of syllables in your name. Was your partner correct? Take turns.**

Pronunciation of the Plural Form

When you say most plural forms, you do not add an extra syllable. But you do add an extra syllable for some plural forms. Add an extra syllable (it sounds like /iz/*) when words end in the following sounds:

Sound	Examples	
/s/	price—prices	dress—dresses
/sh/	dish—dishes	wish—wishes
/ch/	watch—watches	lunch—lunches
/j/	page—pages	age—ages
/ks/	box—boxes	tax—taxes
/z/	nose—noses	size—sizes

1 Listen. Your teacher will read some plural words. Check (✓) the correct box for each word.

1. ☐ no extra syllable
   ☐ extra syllable

2. ☐ no extra syllable
   ☐ extra syllable

3. ☐ no extra syllable
   ☐ extra syllable

4. ☐ no extra syllable
   ☐ extra syllable

5. ☐ no extra syllable
   ☐ extra syllable

6. ☐ no extra syllable
   ☐ extra syllable

7. ☐ no extra syllable
   ☐ extra syllable

8. ☐ no extra syllable
   ☐ extra syllable

9. ☐ no extra syllable
   ☐ extra syllable

2 Work with a partner. One person reads the words in column one aloud. The other person reads the words in column two aloud. Decide together which words have an extra syllable and which ones do not.

One	Two
1. tables	1. dishes
2. lunches	2. sales
3. glasses	3. waves
4. shoes	4. matches

*/ / We use slashes to talk about sounds.

Spelling of the Plural Form

1. Add -*s* to most words.
   book + s = books   day + s = days

2. Add -*es* to words that end in these letters: *s*, *z*, *sh*, *ch*, and *x*.
   box + es = boxes   dish + es = dishes

3. For words that end with a consonant before -*y*: Change the *y* to *i* and add -*es*.
   baby + s = babies   lady + s = ladies

4. For most words that end in -*f* or -*fe*, change -*f* or -*fe* to -*ves*.
   knife + s = knives   leaf + s = leaves

5. There are also some special plural forms. The following are common ones.
   person—people   tooth—teeth
   woman—women   foot—feet
   man—men   mouse—mice
   child—children   goose—geese

1 Change these words from singular to plural.

spoon _____   shelf _____

wish _____   table _____

dress _____   match _____

baby _____   page _____

price _____   man _____

glass _____   box _____

house _____   tablecloth _____

mouse _____   way _____

Spelling of *-ing* Form

1. Add *-ing* to most verbs.
   work + ing = working
   carry + ing = carrying

2. If a verb ends in *-e*, drop the *-e*. Then add *-ing*.
   write + ing = writing

3. If a verb ends in consonant + vowel + consonant, double the final consonant and add *-ing*.
   sit + ing = sitting

1 Fill in the blanks

Ewa's family ____*is* ____*getting*____ (get) ready for the day.

Mornings are always busy and rushed. Ewa's husband Artur

_____ _____ (shave). Rita _____ _____ (wash) her

face. Monica _____ _____ _____ (put on) her socks.

Ewa and her son Niki are in the kitchen. She _____ _____

(prepare) breakfast for the family. At the moment, she _____

_____ (serve) orange juice. Niki _____ _____ (set) the

table. Right now, he _____ _____ (put) the glasses of orange

juice on the table.

The family _____ _____ (try) to get to work and school on

time.

Spelling of the Simple Present

Third Person Singular

1. Add -s to most verbs to make the third person singular form.
   She works   He plays

2. Add -es to verbs that end in these letters: s, z, ch, sh, and x.
   She pushes   He fixes

3. For verbs that end in a consonant before -y, change the y to i and add -es.
   She hurries   He worries

4. There are three special forms.
   I do—it does
   I go—she goes
   I have—he has

---

1   Fill in the blanks.

Celia Alvarez ____wants____ (want) to become an engineer. She

_____ (take) classes at Parker Community College. She

_____ (go) there three nights a week. She

_____ (study) hard, she _____ (like) her

classes, and she _____ (do) well in school.

She also _____ (have) two part-time jobs. On weekends,

she _____ (wash) dishes in a restaurant, and she

_____ (help) in the kitchen. During the week, she

_____ (work) in a daycare center. She _____

(watch) the children at the playground, and she _____

(play) with them.

Celia _____ (work) hard. She _____ (dream)

about being an engineer in the future.

Days of the Week, Months, Seasons

Days of the Week

S = Sunday (Sun.)
M = Monday (Mon.)
T = Tuesday (Tues.)
W = Wednesday (Wed.)
T = Thursday (Thurs.)
F = Friday (Fri.)
S = Saturday (Sat.)

Seasons
summer
winter
spring
fall

Weights and Measures

Weight
ounce, pound, ton
16 ounces (oz.) = 1 pound (lb.)
2,000 pounds = 1 ton (tn.)

Liquid and Dry
cup, pint, quart, gallon, teaspoon, tablespoon
2 cups (c.) = 1 pint (pt.)
2 pints = 1 quart (qt.)
4 quarts = 1 gallon (gal.)
3 teaspoons (t.) = 1 tablespoon (T.)

Distance
inch, foot, yard, mile
12 inches (in.) = 1 foot (ft.)
3 feet (ft.) = 1 yard (yd.)
1,760 yards = 1 mile (mi.)

Months
1997

January (Jan.)

S	M	T	W	T	F	S
			1	2	3	4
5	6	7	8	9	10	11
12	13	14	15	16	17	18
19	20	21	22	23	24	25
26	27	28	29	30	31	

February (Feb.)

S	M	T	W	T	F	S
						1
2	3	4	5	6	7	8
9	10	11	12	13	14	15
16	17	18	19	20	21	22
23	24	25	26	27	28	

March (Mar.)

S	M	T	W	T	F	S
						1
2	3	4	5	6	7	8
9	10	11	12	13	14	15
16	17	18	19	20	21	22
23	24	25	26	27	28	29
30	31					

April (Apr.)

S	M	T	W	T	F	S
		1	2	3	4	5
6	7	8	9	10	11	12
13	14	15	16	17	18	19
20	21	22	23	24	25	26
27	28	29	30			

May

S	M	T	W	T	F	S
				1	2	3
4	5	6	7	8	9	10
11	12	13	14	15	16	17
18	19	20	21	22	23	24
25	26	27	28	29	30	31

June

S	M	T	W	T	F	S
1	2	3	4	5	6	7
8	9	10	11	12	13	14
15	16	17	18	19	20	21
22	23	24	25	26	27	28
29	30					

July

S	M	T	W	T	F	S
		1	2	3	4	5
6	7	8	9	10	11	12
13	14	15	16	17	18	19
20	21	22	23	24	25	26
27	28	29	30	31		

August (Aug.)

S	M	T	W	T	F	S
					1	2
3	4	5	6	7	8	9
10	11	12	13	14	15	16
17	18	19	20	21	22	23
24	25	26	27	28	29	30
31						

September (Sept.)

S	M	T	W	T	F	S
	1	2	3	4	5	6
7	8	9	10	11	12	13
14	15	16	17	18	19	20
21	22	23	24	25	26	27
28	29	30				

October (Oct.)

S	M	T	W	T	F	S
			1	2	3	4
5	6	7	8	9	10	11
12	13	14	15	16	17	18
19	20	21	22	23	24	25
26	27	28	29	30	31	

November (Nov.)

S	M	T	W	T	F	S
						1
2	3	4	5	6	7	8
9	10	11	12	13	14	15
16	17	18	19	20	21	22
23	24	25	26	27	28	29
30						

December (Dec.)

S	M	T	W	T	F	S
	1	2	3	4	5	6
7	8	9	10	11	12	13
14	15	16	17	18	19	20
21	22	23	24	25	26	27
28	29	30	31			

Answer Key

This section provides answers for written exercises only. Because of the communicative nature of the oral exercises, many of them will have varied answers. Some possible answers for the oral exercises are included in the *English Connections Book 1 Teacher's Edition*.

Unit 1

Page 3
Exercise 4

1. She
2. He
3. They
4. She
5. He
6. I
   (Answers will vary.)

Page 4
Exercise 5

1. e
2. d
3. n
4. j
5. b
6. s
7. o
8. v

Exercise 7

1. Davis
2. Miller
3. Wilson
4. Jones
5. Smith
6. Johnson

Unit 2

Page 10
Exercise 1

Let me tell you about the people in my English class. They <u>are</u> from many countries. I think I <u>am</u> the only person from the United States. Young-Soon, Ewa, and Sumalee <u>are</u> the women in my class. Young-Soon <u>is</u> from Korea. Ewa <u>is</u> from Poland. Sumalee <u>is</u> from Thailand. Anton, Pedro, Chan, and Abdul <u>are</u> the men in my class. Anton is Russian, Pedro <u>is</u> Peruvian, Chan is Vietnamese, and Abdul <u>is</u> Egyptian. My teacher <u>is</u> from Chicago. My class is fun.

Exercise 2

Answers will vary.

Page 11
Exercise 3

1. I am
2. She's
3. You're
4. He is
5. They're
6. My friend's

Page 12
Exercise 5

1. Sumalee's not from Lampang. She's from Bangkok.
2. Teresa and her mother aren't from San Antonio. They're from El Paso.
3. Pedro's not from Lima. He's from Cuzco.
4. Ewa and her husband aren't from Krakow. They're from Warsaw.
5. Abdul's not from Cairo. He's from Aswan.
6. Anton's not from Moscow. He's from St. Petersburg.

Page 13
Exercise 7

1. Amarillo is in the north.
2. Dallas is in the northeast.
3. Houston is in the southeast.
4. El Paso is in the west.

Page 14
Exercise 9

Women
1. Lien is Chinese.
2. Yukiko and Yumi are Japanese.
3. Guadalupe and Marta are Guatemalan.
4. Judy is American.

Men
1. Armando is Mexican.
2. Paulo and Carlos are Brazilian.
3. Jonas and Ivan are Ukrainian.
4. Mustafa is Syrian.

Page 15
Exercise 12

1. It's hot.
2. She's hungry.
3. She's tired.
4. He's thirsty.
5. She's hot.
6. It's cold.

Page 16
Exercise 13

1. My name is Ho Kim.
2. "Hi, I'm Daniel" is most common, but either answer is OK.
3. Either answer is fine.
4. "I'm from China" is most common, but either answer is OK.

Page 18
Use What You Know

1. New York City's not in New Jersey. It's in New York.
2. Los Angeles isn't in Washington. It's in California.
3. Chicago's not in Michigan. It's in Illinois.
4. Houston's not in Arizona. It's in Texas.

5. Philadelphia's not in New York. It's in Pennsylvania.
6. San Diego's not in Nevada. It's in California.
7. Detroit's not in Illinois. It's in Michigan.
8. Dallas isn't in Florida. It's in Texas.
9. Phoenix isn't in Colorado. It's in Arizona.
10. Seattle's not in Oregon. It's in Washington.

Unit 3

Page 20
Exercise 1
1. Is Guatemala in Central America?
2. Thailand is in Southeast Asia.
3. Poland is next to Ukraine.
4. Is Egypt on the Mediterranean Sea?
5. Is Peru on the Pacific Ocean?
6. Is Uganda in Africa?

Page 21
Exercise 2
1. Yes, they are.
2. No, she's not.
3. Yes, he is.
4. No, they're not.
5. No, he's not.
6. Yes, he is.

Page 23
Exercise 4
hungry
1. sad
2. hungry
3. happy
4. frustrated
5. angry
6. proud

Page 24
Exercise 6
Sumalee: Teresa, tell me about our classmates.
Teresa: OK.
Sumalee: Is Pedro Latin American?
Teresa: Yes, he is.
Sumalee: Is he Colombian?
Teresa: No, he's not. He's from Peru.
Sumalee: Are Chan and Young-Soon Asian?
Teresa: Yes, they are. He's from Vietnam, and she's from Korea.
Sumalee: Is Abdul Egyptian?
Teresa: Yes, he is.
Sumalee: Are you Mexican?
Teresa: No, I'm not. I'm Mexican American. I'm from Texas.

Page 26
Exercise 10
1. 101
2. 5523
3. 9782
4. 2437
5. (213) 443-0910
6. (616) 291-5654
7. 214-40-0239
8. 113-21-5798

Page 27
Exercise 11
Any of the answers are OK.

Page 28
Wrapping Up
Linda: Hi. I'm Linda Jacobs. What's your name?
Sumalee: My name's Sumalee Thanarang.
Linda: Are you Korean?
Sumalee: No, I'm not. I'm Thai.

Unit 4

Pages 32–33
Exercise 1
1. b
2. a
3. c
4. e
5. d

Exercise 2
A babysitter is someone who takes care of other people's children.

A janitor is someone who cleans and fixes things in a building.

Pages 34–35

Exercise 3
1. A teacher works in a school.
2. An aide, a nurse, and a doctor all work in a hospital.
3. A hairstylist works in a hair salon, but a barber works in a barbershop.
4. A waiter, a busboy, a cook, and a dishwasher, all work in a restaurant.
5. An electrician, a plumber, a carpenter, an architect, and a painter all work at a construction site.

Page 36
Exercise 4
1. a secretary; a clerk
2. a teacher
3. a hairstylist
4. a carpenter; a plumber; an architect; an electrician
5. a busboy; a cook; a dishwasher; a waiter; a waitress
6. a doctor; a nurse; a nurse's aide

Exercise 5
1. daycare workers
2. nurses
3. student
4. cooks

Exercise 6
1. a truck driver
2. nurses
3. a waitress
4. auto mechanics
5. a carpenter
6. a/an _____
(Answers will vary.)

Exercise 7
1. They are dancers.
2. He is a teacher.
3. They are plumbers.
4. She is a pilot.

Wrapping Up
1. Is she a truckdriver?
2. Are they firefighters?
3. Is she an architect?

Unit 5

Exercise 1
1. This is my book.
2. That's your notebook.
3. This is my pen.
4. That's your folder.
5. This is my piece of paper.
6. This is my eraser.

Exercise 2
1. That is a shelf.
2. Those are desks.
3. This is a blackboard.
4. This is a chair.
5. That is a light. OR Those are lights.
6. That is a clock.

Exercise 6
1. Those pencils are long.
2. That suitcase is light.
3. Those books are new.
4. This problem is easy.
5. This clock is large.

Focus on Vocabulary
1. Open the book.
2. Close the book.
3. Repeat the word. Folder.
4. Listen. This is a folder.
5. Hand in your homework. OR
Turn in your homework.
6. Circle the word.

Exercise 8
1. Those are long pencils.
2. That is a light suitcase.
3. Those are new books.
4. This is an easy problem.
5. This is a large clock.

Wrapping Up
This is a thick notebook. OR This notebook is thick.
1. Those books are thick. OR Those are thick books.
2. This book bag is heavy. OR This is a heavy book bag.
3. These pencils are long. OR These are long pencils.
4. That mouse is small. OR That's a small mouse.

Unit 6

Exercise 3

Things to Cook with	Things to Eat with
stove	dishes
pans	cups
pots	spoons
oven	knives
toaster	glasses
microwave oven	forks
blender	
rice cooker	

Exercise 4
1. Yes, there is.
2. No, there isn't.
3. No, there aren't.
4. No, there aren't.
5. Yes, there are.
6. Yes, there is.
7. Yes, there is.
8. No, there aren't.

Exercise 7
1. spoons
2. cabinet
3. tables
4. coffeemaker
5. dishes
6. glass
7. matches
8. knives

Exercise 8
1. tables
2. forks
3. glasses
4. knives
5. matches
6. tablecloths
7. shelves
8. dishes
9. boxes
10. houses

Page 59
Exercise 10

1. on	7. on
2. on	8. under
3. on	9. next to
4. on	10. on
5. over	11. in front of
6. In front of	12. in
	13. next to

Page 60
Exercise 13
This is Abdul's bathroom. There is a small (sink), a brand-new toilet, a (shower,) and a (medicine cabinet.) There are two (towel racks) next to the (sink,) between the (toilet) and the (sink.) There are (two towels) on the (towel racks.) The (medicine cabinet) is over the (sink,) to the left of the (shower.)

Is *a/an* used the first time? Yes
Is *the* used the first time? No

Page 61
Exercise 14
This is the bathroom in Young-Soon's apartment. There is a large sink, a brand-new toilet, a bathtub, and a mirror. The sink is next to the toilet. The bathtub is to the left of the sink. A towel rack is between the sink and the bathtub. There are four towels on it. There is a bath mat in front of the bathtub.

Page 62
Wrapping Up

1. a	8. next to
2. a	9. the
3. a	10. is
4. on	11. a
5. next to	12. next to
6. is	13. the
7. in	

Unit 7

Page 64
Exercise 1
1. Pedro is Gloria's husband.
2. Pedro is Rosa, Susana, and Juan's father.
3. Pedro is Rosita's grandfather.
4. Pedro is Luis's father-in-law.

Page 65
Exercise 3

1. 16	3. 11
2. 13	4. 18

Page 67
Exercise 4

1. 13 people	4. 4 children
2. 9 adults	5. 1 boy, 3 girls
3. 5 men, 4 women	

Page 67
Exercise 5

1. wife	Gloria
2. daughters	Rosa and Susana
3. son	Juan
4. son-in-law	Luis
5. grandchild	Rosita
6. sister	Maria
7. brother	Alberto
8. niece	Ana
9. nephew	Carlos
10. brother-in-law	Pablo

Exercise 6
Luis is showing his wife Rosa's family tree to some friends from work. He is telling them about Rosa's family. "This is my wife, Rosa, and our baby daughter, Rosita. These are Rosa's parents. This is her mother, Gloria, and this is her father, Pedro. This is her brother, Juan, and this is her sister, Susana. This is her grandmother, her father's mother. This is her aunt, Maria, and this is her uncle, Alberto. The others are her cousins.

Page 68
Exercise 7
Rosa is Pedro's daughter. Luis is her husband, and Rosita is her daughter. Juan is her brother, and Susana is her sister. Pedro and Gloria are her parents.

Luis is Pedro's son-in-law. Rosa is his wife. Gloria is his mother-in-law. Susana is his sister-in-law, and Juan is his brother-in-law. Rosita is his daughter.

Exercise 8
1. Her name is Gloria.
2. His name is Juan.
3. Their names are Rosa and Susana.
4. His name is Luis.
5. Her name is Rosita.
6. Its name is Lorenzo.

Page 70
Exercise 10
your
Who's
They're
whose
their
it's
You're

Page 71
Exercise 11

kind	straight
average height	glasses
thin	intelligent
dark	helpful
short	funny

Page 72

Wrapping Up
1. My father's sister is my <u>aunt</u>.
2. My <u>mother</u> or <u>father's</u> son is my brother.
3. My <u>uncle's</u> son is my <u>cousin</u>. My uncle's daughter is my <u>cousin</u>, too.
4. My <u>daughter's</u> husband is my son-in-law.
5. My son's son is my <u>grandson</u>.
6. My husband's sister is my <u>sister-in-law</u>.
Riddles

Your sister or brother.

Unit 8

Page 74
Exercise 1
1. meat   count   (noncount)
2. mushrooms (count)   noncount
3. tea   count   (noncount)
4. pea pods   (count)   noncount
5. onions   (count)   noncount
6. sugar   count   (noncount)

Page 76
Exercise 3
1. Is there any bread?
   No, there isn't.
2. Are there any limes?
   No, there aren't.
3. Are ther any mushrooms?
   Yes, there are.
4. Is there any sugar?
   No, there isn't.
5. Is there any meat?
   No, there isn't.
6. Are there any pea pods?
   Yes, there are.
7. Are there any menus?
   Yes, there are.
8. Is there any rice?
   yes, there is.

Page 77
Exercise 5
Count nouns lemons, eggs, green
peppers, onions,
green beans,
mushrooms, hot
peppers

Noncount nouns chicken, milk, bread,
lettuce, oil, garlic

Page 78
Exercise 7
1. Push
2. Pick Up Prescriptions Here
3. Pay Here
4. Watch Your Step
5. Pull
6. Fragile: Handle with Care

Page 79
Exercise 8
1. Look out!
   Watch out!
   Be careful!
2. Look out!
   Watch out!
3. Stop!
   Don't do that!
4. Stop!
   Be careful!
   Watch out!
5. Stop!
   Don't touch that!
6. Stop!
   Look out!
   Watch out!

Unit 9

Page 84
Exercise 1
1. It's raining. It's cold.
2. It's windy.
3. It's cloudy.
4. It's cold.
5. It's sunny. It's hot.
6. It's snowing. It's cold.

Page 86
Exercise 4

1. 34	7. 80
2. 65	8. 0
3. 22	9. 7
4. 79	10. 15
5. 50	11. 91
6. 45	12. 100

Page 87
Exercise 6

1. 13	5. 70
2. 16	6. 15
3. 90	7. 40
4. 18	8. 14

Page 88
Exercise 10

1. 6:30 P.M.	7. 5:15 P.M.
2. 7:10 A.M.	8. 6:50 A.M.
3. 8:15 P.M.	9. 7:40 A.M.
4. 11:45 A.M.	10. 10:20 P.M.
5. 12:00 P.M.	11. 12:00 A.M.
6. 3:45 A.M.	12. 3:25 P.M.

Exercise 12

1. It's cool and cloudy. Wear your pants and jacket.
2. It's cold and it's snowing. Wear your coat, hat, and boots.
3. It's warm and sunny. Wear your shorts and T-shirt.
4. It's cool and it's raining. Wear your raincoat and boots.
5. It's very hot and very sunny. You are going to the beach. Wear your bathing suit.

Unit 10

Page 98
Exercise 3

1. Pedro is fixing the car at the auto repair shop.
2. Sumalee is shopping at the shoe store.
3. Chan is choosing vegetables at the grocery store.
4. Ewa is taking her dirty clothes to the dry cleaners.
5. Anton is buying clothes at the department store.
6. Teresa is buying bread at the bakery.
7. Abdul is doing his laundry at the laundromat.
8. Young-Soon is getting gas for the car at the gas station.

Page 99
Exercise 4

1. Fu is depositing a check at the bank.
2. Ewa is paying bills at the currency exchange.
3. Anton is talking to a nurse at the health clinic.
4. Teresa is reading a book at the library.
5. Abdul is mailing a letter at the post office.
6. Pedro is looking at an art exhibit at the museum.
7. Chan is buying popcorn at the movie theater.
8. Young-Soon is playing with her nephew at the playground.

Page 100
Exercise 6

1. No, they're not.
2. No, she's not.
3. No, it isn't.
4. No, he's not.
5. No, they aren't.
6. Yes, he is.

Page 101
Exercise 8

1. What's he doing?

   Where's he doing his laundry?
2. Where is he?

   What is he mailing?
3. What is she buying?

   Where is she buying bread and pastries?

4. What is she paying?

   Where is she paying the bill?

Page 104
Wrapping Up

1. They're not eating. They're talking.
2. He's not talking to a friend. He's listening to the radio.
3. She's not writing. She's eating.
4. It's not sleeping. It's standing up.
5. He's not drinking coffee. He's reading.
6. They're not reading. They're playing cards.

Unit 11

Page 106
Exercise 1

1. I sew neckties every day.
2. She takes out the garbage every week.
3. They recycle cans every month.
4. We walk to school every day.

Page 107
Exercise 2

1. Sun. Mon. Tues. Wed. Thurs. Fri. Sat.
2. Sun. Mon. Tues. Wed. Thurs. Fri. Sat.
3. Tues. Thurs.
4. Mon.
5. Tues. Fri.
6. Mon. Tues. Wed. Thurs. Fri.
7. Mon. Tues. Wed. Thurs. Fri.
8. Mon. Wed. Fri. Sat.
9. Tues. Thurs.
10. Sat.

Page 111
Exercise 9

1. Ewa works every day.
2. Artur doesn't work overtime.
3. They don't go grocery shopping together.
4. They go to the park together.

Unit 12

Page 118
Focus on Vocabulary

1. books
2. music
3. videos
4. soccer matches
5. newspapers
6. the TV

Page 119
Exercise 8

1. Chan sometimes watches TV at night.
2. Pedro sometimes plays the charango in the evening.
3. Young-Soon usually goes jogging in the morning.

4. Ewa never watches boxing matches on TV.
5. Anton usually plays with his children at the park on Sundays.
6. Teresa often takes a walk in her neighborhood in the evening.

Page 120
Exercise 10
1. How often do you play soccer?
2. Where does she play basketball?
3. When does he play volleyball?
4. How often do we go to the beach?
5. How often do they go to the park?
6. Where does she go on Saturdays?

Page 121
Exercise 12
1. Do you ~~like~~ like to classical music?
2. Do you ~~like~~ like ~~to~~ watch TV?
3. Do you like ~~like to~~ play cards?
4. Do you ~~like~~ like to football?
5. Do you ~~like~~ like ~~to~~ sew?
6. Do you like ~~like to~~ paint pictures?
7. Do you like ~~like~~ to visit museums?
8. Do you ~~like~~ like to books?
9. Do you like ~~like to~~ travel?
10. Do you ~~like~~ like to movies?

Page 122
Exercise 13
1. I like to play the guitar.
2. I like to read books.
3. I like to watch TV.
4. I like to listen to music.
5. I like to visit museums.
6. I like to play cards.
7. I like to listen to the radio.
8. I like to swim at the beach.

Page 124
Wrapping Up
Sumalee: What do you do in your free time?
Ewa: Well, I love music.
Sumalee: What kind of music do you like to listen to?
Ewa: I love jazz and blues. I like Louis Armstrong and Billie Holliday.
Sumalee: Do you like Wynton Marsalis?
Ewa: Yes, I do. I think he's great. How about you? What kind of music do you like?

Unit 13

Page 129
Exercise 2
1. He can't drive a car.
2. He can write a work order.
3. He can't climb a ladder.
4. He can fix a lamp.

5. He can't take a shower. OR He can take a shower, if he protects his leg.
6. He can't play soccer.

Page 130
Exercise 3
1. Tony can work long hours.
2. Susana can't come to work early.
3. I can't hear you clearly.
4. They can work overtime today.
5. We can come Monday morning.
6. The doctor can't see you today.

Page 133
Exercise 7
1. her	5. it
2. him	6. her
3. them	7. him
4. it	8. them

Exercise 8
1. it	5. it
2. him	6. it
3. me	7. us
4. her	8. them

Exercise 9
The clinic is busy today. Many people want to see the doctor or the nurse. Many people <u>have</u> colds. Other people <u>have</u> young children who need checkups. A man <u>has</u> a broken leg. Another man <u>has</u> a bad backache. Some people <u>have</u> appointments, but others don't.

Page 134
Exercise 10
1. a stomachache	5. headaches
2. a toothache	6. a cold
3. a fever	7. backaches
4. a cut	8. a burn

Page 135
Exercise 12
1. on December 11	5. at night
2. on Tuesday morning	6. at 3:15
3. in 1968	7. at noon
4. in the winter	8. in August

Exercise 13
1. on	6. at
2. in	7. on
3. on	8. at
4. in	9. on
5. in	

Unit 14

Page 140
Exercise 4
1. No, she wasn't.
2. Yes, she was.
3. No, they weren't.

Page 140
Exercise 5

Teresa: <u>Were you</u> at home last night? I called you but no one answered.

Chan: I <u>was</u> at the mall.

Teresa: Oh. <u>Was it</u> croweded?

Chan: Yes, <u>it was</u>. There <u>were</u> lots of people there.

Teresa: <u>Were</u> lots of things on sale?

Chan: Some things <u>were</u> on sale, but most things <u>were</u> still expensive.

Page 141
Exercise 6

1. $450.00
2. $149.00
3. $345.00
4. $129.00
5. $129,000
6. $3,950
7. $28,599
8. $500,000
9. $1,250,000

Page 142
Exercise 8

1. at
2. on
3. at
4. on
5. in
6. in

Exercise 9

1. X
2. the
3. X
4. X
5. the
6. the

Page 143
Exercise 11

1. a year ago
2. last March
3. last month
4. last Saturday
5. yesterday morning
6. this morning
7. this afternoon
8. now

Unit 15

Page 150
Exercise 3

1. ketchup
2. jelly
3. parsley
4. oil
5. soup
6. butter

Page 152
Exercise 6

1. 2
2. 3 T. (tablespoons)
3. 1 T. (tablespoon)
4. 1 t. (teaspoon)
5. 1
6. ½ t. (teaspoon)

Page 153
Exercise 8

a. These items should be circled.:
beef, onions, sour cream, butter, mushrooms, salt, pepper

b. Questions:
How much beef do you need?
How many onions do you need?
How much sour cream do you need?
How much butter do you need?
How many mushrooms do you need?
How much salt do you need?
How much pepper do you need?

Page 154
Exercise 11

1. Split the banana in half.
2. Add the ice cream.
3. Add the chocolate sauce.
4. Put the whipped cream on top.
5. Add the walnuts.
6. Put the cherry on top.

Appendix

Page 169
Exercise 1

1. class 1
2. pencil 2
3. paper 2
4. eraser 3
5. name 1
6. computer 3

Page 170
Exercise 1

1. extra syllable
2. no extra syllable
3. extra syllable
4. no extra syllable
5. no extra syllable
6. extra syllable
7. extra syllable
8. extra syllable
9. no extra syllable

Page 171
Exercise 1

spoons
wishes
dresses
babies
prices
glasses
houses
mice
shelves
tables
matches
pages
men
boxes
tablecloths
ways

Page 172
Exercise 1

is getting
is shaving
is washing
is putting on
is preparing
is serving
is setting
is putting
is trying

Page 173
Exercise 1

wants
takes
goes
studies
likes
does
has
washes
helps
works
watches
plays
works
dreams